CAMPING BY A BILLABONG

Darwin

NORTHERN TERRITORY

Townsville

QUEENSLAND

WEST AUSTRALIA

SOUTH AUSTRALIA

Brisbane

Geraldton

Tarcoola

NEW SOUTH WALES

Port Macquarie
Newcastle
Sydney
Wollongong

Perth

Adelaide

Deniliquin

VICTORIA

Kyneton   Melbourne

TASMANIA

Macquarie Harbour

Launceston

Hobart

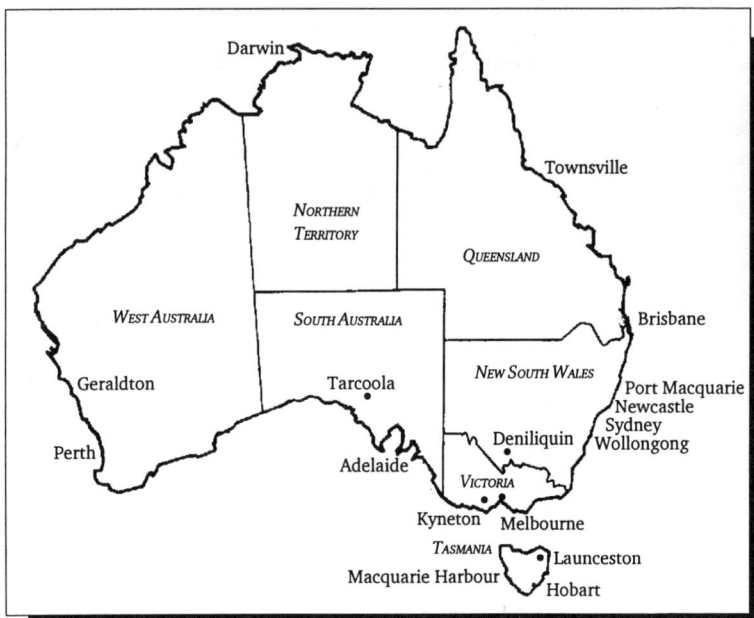

Other Books by Robert French

Gays Between The Broadsheets: Australian Media References
on Homosexuality, 1948-1980 (Sydney, 1986)

'Mossies Could Spread AIDS': Australian Media References
on AIDS, 1981-1985 (Sydney, 1986)

CAMPING BY A BILLABONG

gay and lesbian stories
from Australian history

ROBERT FRENCH

BlackWattle Press
Sydney Australia

For
Garry Wotherspoon

© 1993 Robert French

Published by BlackWattle Press Pty Ltd
PO Box 4, Leichhardt, NSW Australia 2040
November 1993

Printed by Southwood Press, Marrickville NSW

Cover photo: Boys at Swimming Hole, c.1910, Battye Library

ISBN 1 875243 14 3

CONTENTS

ABBREVIATIONS

AA	Australian Archives
AONSW	Archives Office of New South Wales
AOT	Archives Office of Tasmania
BL	Battye Library, State Library of Western Australia
ML	Mitchell Library, State Library of New South Wales
NLA	National Library of Australia
PROV	Public Records Office of Victoria
SAQ	State Archives of Queensland
SRSA	State Records of South Australia
SAWA	State Archives of Western Australia

PUBLICATION HISTORY

A version of *Let The Punishment Fit The Crime, Missionary Positions, More Than Just Friends? The Murder Of Stoker Riley* and *Gentlemen, I Am A Homosexual* first appeared in *OutRage*, while an earlier version of *Coming Out, Ready Or Not* appeared in *Campaign*.

All other chapters first appeared as installments of my column 'In the Past Lane' published in the *Sydney Star Observer* throughout 1992 and 1993.

Kitty & Nancy, Polly, Sally & Bet, To Have & To Hold and *King Of The West End* contain extracts from *A Sodom in the South: Australian Gay History 1787 to 1970* by Garry Wotherspoon and Robert French, a slide presentation first developed in 1986.

PICTURE CREDITS

Cover photograph: BL; Page 8, unknown source; Page 14, NLA; Page 19, unknown source, AONSW; Page 23, NLA; Page 29, unknown source; Page 38, unknown source; Page 45, ML; Page 47, AONSW; Page 49, Jamie Dunbar; Page 52, SAWA, Page 58, NLA; Page 69, The Adelaide *Advertiser;* Page 72, unknown source; Page 86, Sydney *Sunday Telegraph;* Page 96, Melbourne *Truth;* Page 103, Sydney *Sun;* Page 111, *The Bulletin,* Page 114, Phillip Potter

PREFACE

The genesis of this book lies in a history column — 'In the Past Lane' — which I wrote for the gay and lesbian community newspaper, the *Sydney Star Observer*, during 1992-93. To my delight, the column was subsequently picked up by other papers around Australia — the *Westside Observer* in Perth, *Adelaide GT*, *Queensland Pride* in Brisbane and, in an edited form, *Brother-Sister* in Melbourne. Other pieces first appeared in *Outrage* and *Campaign* magazines.

Thanks are due to Larry Galbraith, Campion Decent, Barbara Farrelly, Malcolm Jones and Stephen Dunne at the *Sydney Star Observer*, Chris Dobney and Martyn Goddard at *OutRage*, and Andrew Creagh at *Campaign*; to Gary Dunne, who suggested the idea for this book and helped edit it, and to Laurin McKinnon who agreed to publish.

Some people have generously allowed me to read and use their research — Walter Fogarty in Sydney, Bruce Baskerville in Perth, Clive Moore in Brisbane and John Austin in Melbourne — while Rob Martin became my tireless research assistant in Adelaide thanks to the generosity of the Parkestone Association which gave me a grant enabling me to employ him.

The staff at several institutions were of enormous assistance — Tim Bryant at the Australian Archives, Melbourne Office, Fiona Burn in Sydney, and Susan Cooke and Moira Smythe in the Canberra Office; Lee McGregor and her staff at the State Archives of Queensland; Fabian Loschiavo at the Archives Office of New South Wales; Margy Burn and her staff at the Mitchell Library in the State Library of New South Wales; Michael Organ at Wollongong University Archives; staff at the Laverton Repository of the Public Records Office of Victoria; Ian Pearce at the Tasmanian State Archives; Judy Jeffrey in State Records of South Australia; Chris Coggin, Kandy Jane Henderson, Ann Gill and other reference staff at the State Archives of Western Australia; and those at the Battye

Library, State Library of Western Australia.

In addition, many friends have offered assistance and advice. Among them are Tom Earls, Bill Little, Robert Johnston, Anne Picot, Malcolm Cowan, Shawn Hollbach, Bill Robson, Garry Simes, Graham Carberry, Jim Wafer, and the late John Lee. Tony Newton and Warwick Hunter helped select photographs.

Robert Aldrich, Sasha Soldatow, Andrew Wilson and Terence Watson critically read the manuscript and offered valuable suggestions. Thanks, however, are especially due to Garry Wotherspoon. It was Garry who first urged me, and gave me the confidence, to write up my research. He remains my best critic. To him I dedicate this small effort with gratitude and in friendship.

Robert French
Redfern
Friday, 1 October 1993

Sodomy To Gay Liberation:
An Introduction

> Gay men and Lesbians — so long denied any history — have
> a special need and claim on historical writing that is at once
> accurate *and* accessible.
>
> Martin Duberman, *Stonewall* (NY, 1993)

Like many gay men at the time, I became fascinated by a series of
twelve history articles, entitled 'Our Gay Heritage', written by Martin
Smith and published in *Campaign* magazine in 1977-78. They were
a source of encouragement and a starting point for my own research.
How disappointing it was when, after hours spent chasing references
and checking quotations, I found many of the claims made in those
pieces to be without apparent foundation. Too many of Martin
Smith's statements — for example, that gay bars and beats existed in
Sydney by the 1830s — are a free and fanciful interpretation of the
sources, often closer to fiction than history.

When I came to write my own column I was determined that the
sources for each instalment be published. The same practice has been
followed with the chapters of this book. I strongly believe that I
should be accountable for my findings and statements. At the same
time, I hope that other researchers will be encouraged to go out and
investigate both my references and the many other sources that are
available for gay and lesbian history in Australia.

My aim is a simple one. It is to bring to light the lives and
experiences of the ancestors of today's gay men and lesbians — in a
sense, the ancestors of our tribe. The primary focus is on those
individuals who either stand out from the rest — often because of
their gutsy and defiant attitudes — or whose stories are noteworthy
because they illustrate an important point or event. Through the
inclusion of quotations from the archival record, I have endeavoured
to allow many of these people to speak for themselves and, where

possible, their photographs have been included.

This, however, is certainly not a 'famous fags' variety of history, so current a couple of decades back, where an attempt is made to justify our present existence through the lives of the 'greats' of the past. Post gay liberation, our lives need no such justification.

My primary concern is with the sexual and cultural practice of people engaging in same-sex activity following European settlement. Same-sex activity did not come to Australia with the white invasion. Anthropological evidence points to institutional arrangements and ritual practice among some Aboriginal groups, though these practices are not the subject of this book.

The majority of the stories contained here are about men. There is little about women for nowhere near enough research has been done on lesbians in our past. The stories of those lesbians I have come across have been included.

Because of legal restrictions placed upon their sexual activity, men who had sex with other men feature more prominently within official records, particularly in court records. While these records are a primary source they, in themselves, raise a difficulty and skew the overall picture. They give evidence of people who were caught, often because their crime was the result of coercion or assault (or of activity carried out with a minor). Without a substantial body of personal records, a general problem in Australian history, we are unable to witness the lives and loves of the many others of 'homosexual' persuasion who have existed in our past.

Mention of court records, of course, raises the topic of the police. Police dealings with homosexual men in particular is a common thread within this book. Other threads are the phenomenon of cross-dressing, both male and female, and the kinds of social activity individuals and groups participated in. Another is the manner in which same-sex activity was reported and analysed by the courts, the press and others in authority. All of this gives hint of a rich vein of cultural history waiting to be opened up by further research.

I see the history of same-sex activity in Australia falling into a framework of several stages of identity. It is against this framework the stories in this book need to be seen.

First, there is the era of the Sodomites. Until about the middle of the nineteenth century, the archival records from a number of convict settlements around Australia point to a high level of sexual activity. This activity, however, rather than illustrating the conscious adoption of an identity or lifestyle, has much to do with the situational homosexuality of prison life. Nonetheless, given that prison life was the common state of many people in the colonies for a long time, a range of sexual/emotional relationships could be expected to develop including genuine loving relationships.

There is also evidence, especially from the female factories of Tasmania, of a similar stage of identity for women, but exactly how these women described themselves I do not know.

Outside convict ranks in colonial society there is no evidence of the existence among men, even in embryo form, of a 'Molly Culture' as existed in London from the mid-eighteenth century. At the same time, the sexual lives of women are generally hidden from us. One is left to speculate if same-sex activity may lie behind some of the Romantic Friendships between women of the late nineteenth and early twentieth century.

For men in the same period, court records reveal the existence of a male Beat Culture in the major urban areas. Beats, to use the Australian parlance, were meeting places. They were also the places where men were apprehended engaging in same-sex activity. Many beats, still important in male homosexual culture in Australia today, have a long and continuous history of activity. The existence of a beat culture publicly signals the beginnings of a homosexual sub-culture and, certainly, by the early twentieth century but possibly even earlier, some of the men who 'did the beats' had come to identify themselves as 'homosexual'.

The 1920s saw well-established Homosexual Sub-cultures in the major cities all over Australia. While there were recognised bars and coffee shops where people could discretely gather, most social activity centred on private parties. In the large cities of Melbourne and Sydney, evidence points to the emergence of these homosexual sub-cultures earlier in the century, but it is difficult to be too specific about this. Importantly, these sub-cultures included women who seem for the first time to identify themselves as 'lesbian'.

It is at this point that printed evidence other than court reports becomes available including published reminiscences and the sensationalist reports in the pages of scandal sheets and the 'yellow press'.

By the post-war period, the homosexual sub-cultures had grown into a vigorous, but still closeted, Camp Scene of homosexual men and lesbians with its own established rituals and rites such as 'camp weddings'. In some cities, there began to develop a commercial homosexual scene with pubs, bars and coffee lounges specifically catering to a camp clientele. Also, by the late 1960s, there were active social groups in all the major cities but in Australia there was nothing equivalent to the homophile groups of the United States or the political lobbying groups of the United Kingdom.

Finally in 1970, with the formation of the first openly homosexual organisations around Australia, we see the beginnings of the Gay and Lesbian Communities we know today.

My interests in this book are with sodomites, homosexuals, lesbians and camp people up to the period of gay liberation but not beyond. The stories can be seen as illustrating themes of importance to our history and sense of identity, even when written around a particular incident or person. I have resisted the temptation to open out the chapters and to write a more detailed history of homosexuals and homosexuality in Australia. That will be the task of another publication.

FOR SOURCES ON GAY AND LESBIAN HISTORY IN AUSTRALIA, SEE:
Robert French, 'Where the Action Was: Archival Sources for Gay History in Australia' in Robert Aldrich and Garry Wotherspoon (ed), *Gay Perspectives: Essays in Australian Gay Culture* (Sydney, 1992)
Craig Johnston and Robert Johnston, 'The Making of Homosexual Men' in Verity Burgmann and Jenny Lee, *Staining the Wattle*, (Melbourne, 1988)
ON ENGLAND'S MOLLY CULTURE, SEE:
Rictor Norton, *Mother Clap's Molly House: the Gay Subculture in England, 1700 - 1830* (London, 1992)
ON EMERGING SUBCULTURES IN AUSTRALIA, SEE:
Garry Wotherspoon, *City of the Plain: History of a Gay Subculture* (Sydney, 1991)
John Lee, 'Male Homosexual Identity and Subculture in Adelaide before World War II' in Robert Aldrich and Garry Wotherspoon, *op cit*
Dino Hodge, *Did You Meet Any Malagas? A Homosexual History of Australia's Northernmost Capital* (Darwin, forthcoming)
Clive Moore, 'That Abominable Crime: First Steps Towards a Social History of Male Homosexuals in Colonial Queensland, 1859-1900' in Robert Aldrich (ed), *Gay Perspectives II* (Sydney, forthcoming)
Graham Carberry, 'Some Melbourne Beats: A Map of a Sub Culture from the 1930s to the 1950s' in Robert Aldrich and Garry Wotherspoon, *op cit*

LET THE PUNISHMENT FIT THE CRIME

When Captain Arthur Phillip stepped ashore at Camp Cove, at the entrance to Sydney Harbour, on 22 January 1788, he would hardly have envisaged the type of diverse society which was to grow out of the convict settlement he was about to found and govern.

It is certain that Phillip, generally regarded as a product of the European Enlightenment, could not have foreseen that such a society would comprise recognised communities of gay men and lesbians. After all, the concepts of 'homosexuality' and of 'the homosexual' were not to be conceived of for another eighty-one years, and gay liberation lay a further hundred years beyond that.

Phillip, of course, shared the prejudices of his time in his attitude toward men whom he thought of as 'sodomites'. (Women as people with sexual feelings, let alone as lesbians, I imagine would have been beyond his imagination.) Hence, on 28 February 1787, he could write to the Colonial Secretary, Lord Sydney, in London that, in the new colony —

> There are two crimes that would merit death — murder and sodomy. For either of these crimes I would wish to confine the criminal till an opportunity offered of delivering him as a prisoner to the natives of New Zealand, and let them eat him. The dread of this will operate much stronger than the fear of death.

Perhaps Phillip need not have worried, for during the period of his governorship, as Captain Watkin Tench tells us, no such crimes occurred —

> If it be recollected how large a body of these people are now congregated, in the settlement of Port Jackson, and at Norfolk Island, it will, I think, not only excite surprise, but afford satisfaction, to learn, that in the period of four years few crimes of a deep dye, or a hardened nature have been perpetrated: murder and unnatural sins rank not hitherto in

the catalogue of their enormities.

In the light of later knowledge, this can only be seen as a statement of extreme naivety. Later court cases and the resultant executions give ample evidence of the great amount of same-sex activity occurring among the men.

It will surprise many that the first recorded execution for sodomy took place as far back as 1727 — sixty-one years before Captain Phillip landed at Sydney with his first fleet of British convicts.

In that year, the Dutch ship *Zeewijk* foundered on what is now known as Gun Island in the Pelsaert Group of the Houtman Abrolhos off present day Geraldton, Western Australia. The survivors, under their Captain, Jan Steyns, spent the next nine months building a new sixteen-metre-long vessel which, when completed in March 1728, was used to sail from the island.

The one dark event of this heroic tale of survival occurred on 2 December 1797. Two young sailors, Adriaan Spoor and Pieter Engelse were accused, tried and found guilty of sodomy. Sentenced to death, they were exiled to separate smaller islands without food or water. As Edward Duyk states in his book, *The Dutch in Australia*, 'Death must have been slow and full of torment'.

Adriaan and Pieter are our first martyrs. But there were to be others.

British law required the sentence of death to be passed following a conviction for buggery. However, in the United Kingdom, as Jeffrey Weeks has stated —

The death penalty for buggery, tacitly abandoned after 1836, was finally abolished in England and Wales in 1861 ... to be replaced by penal servitude of between 10 years and life.

This certainly was the practice followed in later Australian colonies, but executions actually did take place in the colonies of New South Wales and Van Diemen's Land. As far as I can ascertain, there were at least four in Sydney between 1828 and 1839 and at least thirteen in Hobart and Launceston from 1828 until 1863. It is worth noting that executions continued in Van Diemen's Land decades after they had ceased in England.

The first trial for sodomy took place in Sydney in 1796, though the records for the case seem not to have survived. Francis Wilkinson was accused of buggering a fellow settler but was acquitted.

The first person to be hanged for sodomy in the colony was

Alexander Brown in 1828. The offence occurred between Brown and a young man, who from the evidence seems to have been a willing enough partner, while both were at sea. The young man's death sentence was commuted.

Most of the trials for sodomy up to 1856, the first year of responsible government in New South Wales, were in the 1830s. Walter Fogarty, in his 1989 History thesis, *Indecent Connection* explains that the alteration in —

the general sentencing pattern of the colonial courts ... [is] the result of a disciplinary push by the government prompted by the growth in the convict population.

Of the dozen or so cases up to 1839 it is worth noting that some were for offences committed with boys, and some instances obviously were rape. We should not fall into the trap of thinking all who died were 'martyrs'.

The last person to be executed for sodomy in Sydney was Thomas Parry in 1839. Again, while the *Sydney Morning Herald* records on 19 August that 'He had sentence of death passed on him', no court records survive on his case.

In the colony of Van Diemen's Land (which became known as Tasmania in 1856) there was a much higher incidence of execution for sodomy. This, perhaps, is not surprising given its status as the penal colony for the other Australian colonies. Life for a convict there was generally a good deal harsher and more wretched than elsewhere.

The first sodomy trial would seem to have been of Samuel Cox in 1828. He was charged with —

Feloniously assaulting James Steadman a youth [about] the age of 16 years and against the order of nature having a venereal affair and carnally knowing him, and feloniously committing with him that detestable and abominable crime of buggery (not to be named among Christians).

As Steadman was not similarly charged, he may have been an unwilling participant. The sentence of death was duly passed and, presumably, Cox was executed though I cannot find any record of it.

The last two executions for sodomy in Tasmania took place in 1863. Heindrick Whitnalder was hanged in Hobart, while Denis Collins, in Launceston, was the last person to be executed for buggery in the Australian colonies.

Finally, it should not be assumed that those who had their

sentences commuted to a term in prison were in any way the lucky ones. Prison life was a mixed blessing indeed as the case of John Wilson (discussed in a later chapter) clearly illustrates. He was sentenced to death in Melbourne in 1863 and the sentence was commuted to life in prison. His subsequent short life was appalling in the extreme. The first six years in prison were spent in chains. He lived only another three years, dying of 'brain fever' in 1869. In comparison, being sent to New Zealand would have been a kinder fate.

SOURCES: Governor Phillip to Lord Sydney, 28 February 1787 *Historical Records of New South Wales* Vol. 1, Part 2, pp. 52-3

Watkin Tench, *A Complete Account of the Settlement at Port Jackson* (London, 1793) p. 205

Edward Duyk, *The Dutch in Australia* (Melbourne, 1987) p. 26

Walter Fogarty, *Indecent Connection: Notions of the Development of the Homosexual in New South Wales Law, 1788 — 1900* BA (Hons) Thesis in History, University of New South Wales

AONSW. Police Magistrates Bench and the Central Criminal Court, Depositions, 1809 — 1939

AOT. SC41, Record Books of persons tried in Criminal Sessions of the Supreme Court, 1824 — .

KITTY & NANCY, POLLY, SALLY & BET

The early colonies of New South Wales and Van Diemen's Land were known generally for the laxity of their so-called 'moral' arrangements. Prostitution was common and even high officials often chose looser-than-conventional arrangements. For example, Governors Phillip and King in Sydney had mistresses, as did Lieutenant-Governors Collins and Sorell in Hobart.

Marriage was not a popular institution. In 1810 there had been one hundred and eighty-one marriages, in 1813, fifty-two, and in 1817, forty-seven. Whatever today's moralists might like us to believe about the eternal nature of the nuclear family, there is very little evidence of it in white Australia's early history.

The probable extent of same-sex activity that had been occurring in the Australian colonies was really only first indicated in the 1830s by the evidence given before a British Parliamentary Committee, the *Select Committee ... [on] Transportation [and] its Influence on the Moral State of Society in the Penal Colonies*, usually called the Molesworth Committee. A variety of witnesses gave evidence on the prevalence of immorality in the colony and speculated on the level of 'unnatural acts' that occurred there.

Surprisingly, the Chief Justice in the Colony of New South Wales, Sir Francis Forbes, a witness at the inquiry, admitted that the colony 'had been called a Sodom in the papers', but he didn't think that sodomy was common. Other witnesses, particularly in relation to the convict population, strongly disagreed.

A magistrate, James Mudie, was able to supply more detail than his legal superior. He elaborated on the possible prevalence of same-sex activity among the convict population, particularly on Norfolk Island. When asked about the frequency of unnatural offences in the colonies, Mudie replied that it was common.

Other witnesses similarly testified. However, one colonist, Mr Slade, thought that it was only confined to the lower class of convicts. He believed that 'among gentlemen convicts it would excite abhorrence!'

Evidence was also given as to the supposedly greater frequency of same-sex activity in Australia compared with England. When another witness was asked how common sodomy was in the colonies, he replied 'I should say that there were 100 cases in Sydney to one in the United Kingdom.'

Some of the most detailed evidence is that of the Roman Catholic Vicar-General of New Holland and Van Diemen's Land, Bishop William Ullathorne. The Bishop was a veritable goldmine of information about convicts and convict life. (Did he gain this information from the confessional?)

He noted that the crimes were particularly common among stockmen in country districts, as well as being rife in the convict establishments both on the mainland and in the outpost of Norfolk Island and the colony of Van Diemen's Land. This is the first evidence we have of same-sex activity outside convict ranks.

He also thought that the Aborigines were ignorant of homo-eroticism. When he was asked about conditions in the colonies, particularly about 'unnatural acts', the Bishop noted that those crimes were unknown to 'the savage' until they were taught them by the convict. We know this to be false. Anthropological evidence points to institutional arrangements and ritual practice among some of the native groups. These ranged from permissive sexual arrangements between a man and his wife's brother (since the latter belonged to the same marriage class as his wife) to men masturbating each other before setting out on a warrior mission.

One of Ullathorne's great concerns was with the moral contamination of the young. He laid much emphasis on the way in which boys and young men became educated about 'unnatural activities'. The corruption of youth was also a concern of James Mudie and he also held the common misconception that the young were inculcated into the vice.

Mudie's evidence is interesting, since, in passing, he gives a glimpse of several aspects of same-sex behaviour. For example, he tells of the taking on of female attributes, female names, and of female attitudes to same-sex activity. He adds that he had heard a number of very horrid stories 'if a boy happens to be upon a farm, and to be sent to the prisoners' barracks in Sydney, the boys will go by the names of Kitty and Nancy.'

James Barnes elaborated upon this phenomenon. When giving evidence about Macquarie Harbour prison settlement on the remote western coast of Van Diemen's Land, he pointed out that the female names were usually attributed to the 'passive' partner —

Several individuals in the settlement went by female names ... so common was the practice at the settlement during the period of 1827, that many convicts went by the names of Polly, Sally, Bet, etc. to designate the individuals upon whom those crimes were supposed to be committed.

Did these people use these names to refer to themselves? Was the usage common or, even, a form of abuse? We probably will never know for sure.

The good Bishop, when asked how sodomy was generally viewed by the population, thought that it probably was regarded with great distaste by the mass of the population, and even most convicts.

When further asked why, if there was so much sodomy and moral pollution in the colonies, there were so few indictments and convictions, the Bishop replied that there were difficulties in getting people to act as witnesses — indeed, the general populace were reluctant to 'dob in' their mates! Or, as I suspect, did so only when rape, or perhaps jealousy, was involved.

Other witnesses before the Inquiry refer to the use of the term 'sod' though, again, we can't be sure if it was used as a term of affection or abuse. Probably both.

Just how the sodomites categorised themselves, if ever they did, is hard to determine as almost nothing in the way of personal records have survived. The law and the church told them they were sodomites and sinners, these were the concepts that were brought by the authorities to Australia, so presumably this is how they were conditioned to think of themselves.

Nonetheless, despite being classed in this way, some convicts do seem to have derived a little pleasure from their colonial experience.

SOURCE: *Report from the Select Committee on Transportation,* UK Parliamentary Papers, 1837 and 1838

FOR A DISCUSSION ON ABORIGINAL SEXUALITY, SEE: Jim Wafer, et al, 'Peopling the Empty Mirror: The Prospects for Lesbian and Gay Aboriginal History' in Robert Aldrich (ed), *Gay Perspectives II* (Sydney, forthcoming)

AND SO TO BED

References to lesbians or to women having sex with other women appear infrequently in the official archives of this country. One obvious factor is the non-illegality of their sexual activity which kept them from the reach of the law enforcers, whose records have provided gay researchers with a treasure trove of material. One net effect of this, of course, has been the difficulty in locating material, and very little has yet been researched by lesbians themselves.

One interesting story — the only one I know where two women were faced with a charge of indecency — has been put on record. It occurred at the Female Factory in Hobart in 1843 and appears as part of the evidence given to a Committee of Inquiry into female prisons.

The committee, consisting of the Colonial Treasurer and four other eminent persons (all male, of course), was commissioned by the Governor of Van Dieman's Land in 1841 to inquire into Female Convict Discipline. Some of what they were told over the three years of their investigation — while presented in a negative light — does give illustration to the prevailing attitudes to female sexuality in the nineteenth century.

In investigating the Female Factories of Launceston and Hobart, plenty of evidence was gathered on what the Committee's Report describes as 'the inevitable tendency of confinement ... to produce a deterioration of morals'.

The Superintendent at Hobart observed in his evidence on the behaviour of convict women. 'They corrupt each other. Their conversation turns upon obscenity and drinking. Their songs sometimes are disgusting'.

Indeed, on one occasion 'two women had recently been detected in the very act of exciting each others persons — on the Lord's Day and in the House of God — and at the very time divine service was performing'.

Well it was a kind of worship I suppose — and, one hopes, a divine experience!

The situation was apparently worse, even dangerous, in the Launceston Factory. As John Hutchinson, the Superintendent, reported —

> At present if anything be wrong it is dangerous to go among the large number in the room ... I have been set defiance when I have wanted to take out a woman from the ward, and am obliged to carry pistols ... I have had the shirt torn from my back ... Their conduct generally is most depraved and disgusting and their language most obscene, unnatural intercourse between them is carried on to a great extent.

The Female Factory, Hobart

He related one incident that illustrated his concerns. Following a complaint, he went to the ward and there saw five women —

> dancing perfectly naked and making obscene attitudes towards each other, they were singing and shouting and making use of most disgusting language.

To our ears, it may sound more like a pleasure playground, but remember that conditions in the Van Dieman's Land female factories, particularly in the Hobart Factory located in the dank Cascades gully, were harsh and squalid. The death rate was far in excess of a similar institution at Parramatta, New South Wales.

It is in this environment that the story of Jane Owen and Eliza Taylor is set. Each was an inmate of the Hobart Factory. Jane Owen had the misfortune to share her hammock, not uncommon in colonial prisons, with Ann Fisher, who was a wards-woman and therefore a person with a little authority.

One night Eliza Taylor came into the hammock shared by Fisher and Owen. She and Owen talked together in an 'indecent' manner, with obscene suggestions, until near dawn. They apparently supposed Fisher to be asleep.

The following evening Owen invited Taylor to her hammock and, as Fisher recounts it, 'They conversed together in a very indecent way and after some time ... Taylor asked Owen to give her that [which] she asked her for the night before.'

After some further discussion 'Owen said to Taylor that she never had been nailed.' Fisher then explains in the evidence that 'the expression they mean by nailing is indecently using their hands with each others persons.' She goes on further that 'Taylor and Owen did behave on that night in a way I have described. Owen made use of her hands on the person of Taylor indecently' and 'they behaved in this indecent manner for four or five minutes.' After this, Fisher left the bed and 'called Taylor a nasty beast.'

Wards-woman Fisher reported the incident the following morning. As a consequence, Taylor and Owen were charged with gross indecency. With no other evidence except that provided by Fisher, the charge was found to be not proved. This did not prevent Owen and Taylor being subsequently held in solitary confinement lest they corrupt others.

SOURCE: AOT. Colonial Secretary's Office. CSO22/50, Correspondence files. *item*: Report and Evidence of the Committee of Inquiry into Female Convict Discipline, 1841-1843

TO HAVE AND TO HOLD

It surprises many to learn that there is evidence of men actually establishing relationships, which we would now class as homosexual, back into the nineteenth century and even as far back as the convict period. As previously noted, many of these liaisons were the result of what is referred to as situational homosexuality.

Nonetheless, they could not all have been so. Take the following extract from the 1846 report of Magistrate Robert Pringle Stuart into the penal colony on Norfolk Island. He goes one night to visit the convict barracks —

> On the doors being opened, men were scrambling into their own beds from others, in a hurried manner, concealment being evidently their object. It was evident that wardsmen, not being liable to supervision, nor having any external support, did not exercise any authority and were mere passive spectators of irregularity, which prevails here at night to an enormous amount ... I entertain no doubt that atrocities of the most shocking, odious character are there perpetrated, and that unnatural crime is indulged in to excess ...
>
> I am told, and I believe, that upwards of 100 — I have heard as many as 150 — couples can be pointed out, who habitually associate for this most detestable intercourse, and whose moral perception is so completely absorbed that they are said to be 'married', 'man and wife', etc ... It is lamentable to observe that the natural course of affection is quite distracted and that these parties manifest as much eager earnestness for the society of each other as [for] members of the opposite sex ...
>
> On the Sunday before I embarked, a convict from Van Diemen's Land was detected during the hours of Divine Service in the afternoon in the company of a lad from

England, within the outer enclosure of the new gaol, with their clothes down; their position left no doubt about their purpose.

Were it not for the harsh conditions under which they existed, one almost gets the impression of Norfolk Island as a gay pleasure resort.

Then there is the brief love letter originally found among the possessions of a convict who was executed in 1846 (and recently re-discovered by Ian Brand in the Archives Office of Tasmania). It is a touching memorial of this unnamed writer's love for a fellow prisoner, Jack, and of his concern at having to leave his lover behind —

> Dear Lover,
> I hope you wont forget me when i am far away and all my bones is moulded away I have not closed an eye since i have lost sight of you your precious sight was always a welcome and loving charming spectacle. Dear Jack I value Death nothing but it is in leaving you my dear behind and no one to look after you But I hope you will beware of the delusive of man. the only thing that grieves me love is when i think of the pleasant nights we have had together. I hope you wont fall in love with no other man when i am dead
> I remain your True and loving affectionate Lover.

Other records, also found among official sources, indicate explicit homosexual relationships. The 1878 prison correspondence of the bushranger Captain Moonlite (George Scott), discovered by Garry Wotherspoon in the Archives Office of New South Wales, tells of Scott's friendship with one of the gang members, James Nesbit, and of his grief at the death of his companion in their final shoot-out with the police following the seizure of a sheep at Wantabadgery in southern New South Wales. One writer has described what happened after Nesbit was shot —

> Heedless of the firing, he [Scott] covered the face ofone of the fallen men [Nesbit] with his handkerchief, stooped, raised the wounded man, got under him and, carrying him over his shoulder, made for the house, from which the other three bushrangers kept up a straggling fire.

Another writer takes up the description of what happened inside the house. As Nesbit lay dying, 'his leader wept over him like a child,

Captain Moonlite and James Nesbit

laid his head upon his breast, and kissed him passionately'.

Nesbit died and Scott was taken prisoner. He was tried, found guilty, convicted and sentenced to death. Throughout his time in prison, he wore a ring made from a lock of Nesbit's hair. His major concern in his last few days of life was to ensure his burial arrangements. He wanted to be buried in the same grave as Nesbit and his desired inscription for their joint tombstone seems to say it all —

Sadly, Nesbit's remains are buried near where he died while Scott is buried in Sydney's Rookwood necropolis.

From all the evidence, it is difficult not to believe that the relationship was homo-erotic, or even explicitly sexual.

Many other couples suffered for their friendship. Take the

example of John Boyd and William Reily. They were both living (in separate rooms) in the North Australia Hotel in Townsville in 1886. Unfortunately for them, a detective, Richard Dyer, also boarded in the hotel, and they had aroused his suspicion. One Sunday morning at 1 am, he and two others followed the couple along the beach. Eventually they came upon them fucking in a secluded area. Dyer crept up to them and —

> found the prisoner Reily was lying on his belly on the ground and the prisoner Boyd was lying on him. I could hear the prisoner Reily grunting or moaning ... with my right hand I shoved down between the privates of the prisoner Boyd and the fundament of the prisoner Reily. I there found the prisoner Boyd's privates which was quite rigid and inserted in the prisoner Reily's fundament. The prisoner Boyd's penis was greasy.

The law required proof of anal penetration before a conviction could be gained. Boyd, as the active partner in 'the crime', got three years' hard labour, while Reily was given two years. These were typical sentences for the time.

We know of these people because their illegal sexual activities came into contact with the law. As yet we know little of those nineteenth century male couples, and there surely were many, who escaped official detection and managed to live reasonably fulfilling lives together.

SOURCES: E. F. (ed), *Norfolk Island — The Accounts of Robert Pringle Stuart and Thomas Begley Naylor* (Sullivans Cove, Hobart, 1978)

Ian Brand, *The Convict Probation System: Van Diemen's Land, 1839-1854* (Hobart, 1990) p. 102. For the original letter in AOT, see: Governor's Office. GO 33/57, Despatches p. 251, Civil Commandant to Comptroller General, 7 October 1846

SAQ. Supreme Court Briefs and Depositions, 1858 — . CCT 7/N30, Townsville. *item*: John Boyd and William Reily, 1890

Garry Wotherspoon, 'Moonlite and ... Romance? The Death-cell Letters of Captain Moonlite and Some of their Implications', *Journal of the Royal Australian Historical Society*, Vol. 78 Nos. 3 and 4, 1992. For the original records in AONSW, see: Colonial Secretary. Special Bundle, Letters of Scott and Rogan 1878-79, and Clerk of the Peace. 9/6643, Central Criminal Court Depositions. *item*: Regina v Scott, December 1879

MISSIONARY POSITIONS

The sometimes popular orgasmic exclamation, Oh God! presumably takes on a mixed meaning for clergymen who happen to be homosexual. There have been a number of them who feature in our history.

The Reverend Samuel Perry Allen was a school master at Riversdale House in Adelaide in 1854. He found himself before the courts on a charge that he did 'stir up and excite' in the mind of Albert Lamont, a pupil —

> filthy lewd and unchaste desires and inclinations ... did unlawfully wickedly deliberately [sic] and wilfully counsel solicit and require the said Albert Lamont to expose [his] private parts ... and did ... lay hold of and rub and irritate the private parts of the same Albert Lamont ... and did ... require the same ... to lay hold of and rub and irritate the private parts of him the said Samuel Allen to the great displeasure of Almighty God and to the great scandal of all humankind and Against the peace of our Lady the Queen her Crown and Dignity.

For this, and a charge for a similar offence with another fifteen-year-old student, Allen received four years' hard labour. The scandal of it all rocked the staid Adelaide establishment for many more years than that.

The most 'notorious' case, however, is that of the Reverend William Yate.

In June 1836 the *Prince Regent* sailed into Port Jackson from England. On board was the Reverend William Yate, a member of the conservative evangelical Church Missionary Society. He was returning to the New Zealand Missions after a short and very successful lecture tour in London and Cambridge. Yate, however, never reached New Zealand, for within six months he had sailed back to England under a cloud of scandal.

Yate had been a missionary in New Zealand since 1828 and had made many previous trips to the Australian colonies, successfully preaching and collecting for his own mission station in the Bay of Islands. While in England, in 1835, he had gained fame as a preacher, even being given an audience with King William IV. His lectures and publications, however, not only emphasised his own work, but gave much credit to the Maoris for the construction of a new Christian civilisation in formerly 'pagan' New Zealand. All this was to the annoyance of, and led to some bitterness and resentment on the part of, his fellow missionaries.

Upon Yate's arrival in Sydney, the head of the Anglican church, Bishop Broughton, sought leave for him from Samuel Marsden, local head of the Church Missionary Society. Broughton wanted Yate to act as a temporary preacher in Sydney. The approval being given, Yate immediately began to cut a dashing figure in Anglican church circles. His fiery sermons, particularly directed against the Roman Catholic school system, brought him into favour, especially with the Bishop, who was in dispute with Governor Bourke over concessions to the Roman Catholic church. Imagine Broughton's dismay when disturbing allegations were levelled against his new-found supporter.

On the voyage out to Australia, Yate had been accompanied by his sister and a fellow missionary, the Reverend Richard Taylor. According to later testimony, Taylor and another passenger had been scandalised by Yate's behaviour on board ship. Yate had spent part of the voyage in the company — and hammock — of the third mate, Edwin Denison. Further, after their arrival in Sydney, Yate moved into lodgings with Denison in Park Street. Neighbours soon complained to Taylor about Yate's behaviour.

A third young man, and fellow seaman of Denison, (the wonderfully named) Dick Deck, joined them in their bed, though Deck later commented that 'there had been so much tickling that [he] was obliged to get out of bed and sleep on a sofa in the next room in order to obtain any rest.'

In mid-August, Taylor confided his information to a horrified Marsden, who in turn directed him to the Bishop. Broughton immediately confronted the young missionary, who denied any scandalous conduct whatsoever. The Bishop, however, did not believe him. He relieved Yate of his preaching duties and handed the problem over to Marsden, as local head of the Church Missionary Society. He also warned Yate that if he continued to remain in Sydney he would be forced to convene a church court to hear formally the allegations against him.

Marsden gave Yate the choice of either appearing before a tribunal in order to clear his name, or of sailing immediately for

Reverend William Yate

England. At first Yate opted for the latter course of action, but then, as A. T. Yarwood, Marsden's biographer, states 'he changed his mind shrewdly anticipating that his accusers had insufficient evidence to sustain their charges'.

Ironically, the most damaging evidence against Yate were the letters which Denison had sent to him and which Yate, in the belief that they showed the innocence of his friendship with Denison, had given to Broughton. In one of them Denison had spoken of the 'melancholy pleasure' of sitting on a sofa beside Yate while the latter prepared his sermons. In another, Denison pleaded with Yate 'not to forget the promise you had made me one night whilst lying in your hammock on board the *Prince Regent*, viz: to make mention of me often in your prayers'.

The matter dragged on for some months without resolution, while Marsden became increasingly unpopular in church circles. His behaviour seemed to be vindictive against the young missionary, who continued to receive wide support.

Then, in October, came evidence from the New Zealand Missions which was to change the nature of the case entirely. Depositions from six young Maori men described in graphic detail countless acts of mutual masturbation (*titoitoi*) and oral intercourse which Yate had engaged in with them. The deposition of Samuel Kohi is typical —

> He said to me, Pull off your clothes. I said to him, For what purpose? He said to me, That we may copulate. I replied, I do not understand what you are going to do. He said to me, All Europeans act thus while they are single men. Then because they sleep with their wives this practice is left off. But as for me my wife is this, a hand. I said to him, By whom were you taught this practice? He said to me, By my father I was taught this practice in my childhood ...
> On another occasion, when prayers were over while we were at Kerikeri, he said to me, Let us go (you and I) to my store and there we will *titoitoi*. We went there. He said to me, Take hold of my penis, *titoitoia* with your hand. He said to me, Undo the buttons of your trouser. I undid them, he took hold with his hand and I with my hand took hold of his penis, and *titoitoi*. He gave me sixpipes and six figs of tobacco on the Sabbath day, as payment. I went to him three times before my baptism, and since my baptism I have been many times, more than I can count.

It is evident from these depositions that Yate was not above exploiting his position of authority in order to gain sexual favours, which he mostly paid for with tobacco.

It would seem, as well, that his activities had not been confined just to New Zealand. As Taylor wrote in his diary for 25 October 1835, 'He was accused of the same crime at the Tonga Isles, New Zealand, Van Diemen's Land, and every time he visited this colony'.

Still Yate protested his innocence. Finally, Marsden and Broughton decided that the matter should be sent to Francis Fisher, the Crown Solicitor in Sydney, to see if a criminal prosecution could be brought against Yate. To their dismay, he replied in December that 'on perusing these disgusting details it seems more than probable that the crime of sodomy cannot be proved against him according to law'. He urged that more details be sought from New Zealand.

In the meantime, according to Judith Binney, Yate's aggrieved fellow missionaries in New Zealand had taken retribution into their own hands. After a 'solemn day of fasting and humiliation,' they burnt all Yate's goods and possessions and shot his (presumably innocent?) horse.

Yate, no doubt realising that he could not hold out much longer, finally decided to leave the colony. On 17 December 1836, he, his sister and Denison — 'the companion of his disgrace' as Samuel Marsden called him — sailed for England, much to the relief of the Anglican church in Sydney.

Little is known of Yate's later life. In 1843, he applied for the chaplaincy to a workhouse at St James, Westminster. The workhouse board agreed to his appointment after an investigation of his character and of the allegations previously made against him (of which they had little evidence). The Bishop of London, however, refused the appointment.

In 1848 Yate, perhaps appropriately enough, was placed in charge of a mission to seamen at Dover, where according to one source, he is said to have died 'at an advanced age,' and no doubt a happy man!

SOURCES: SASA. GRG 36/1, Indictments and Depositions, 1837-1924 Box 4, December 1854 Samuel Perry Rupert Allen
AONSW Col. Sec. Correspondence. 4/2357.1, 1837 Crown Solicitor — Criminal. item: 36/10481
Judith Binney, 'Whatever Happened to Poor Mr Yate? An Exercise in Voyeurism' The New Zealand Journal of History, Vol. 9 No. 2, 1975
A. T. Yarwood, Samuel Marsden (Melbourne, 1977) pp. 272-4

MORE THAN JUST FRIENDS?

(With Garry Wotherspoon)

Few residents of the present day Brisbane suburb of Herston would be aware of the origins of its name. Fewer still would know that the name memorialises what is possibly one of Queensland's great untold homosexual love stories.

The name Herston is an amalgam, a joining together of the first part of the surname of Robert Herbert, Queensland's first Premier, and the last part of the surname of John Bramston, Herbert's close friend and several times Attorney-General in the Queensland Parliament. The relevance of all this for Australians begins in the 1850s.

By the end of that decade, pressure had built up to create a new colony out of what was then the northern part of New South Wales. This region had recently experienced dramatic growth, with a wealthy pastoral industry and booming mercantile centres at Moreton Bay and other coastal towns. Residents of the north resented the fact that political and economic control of their lives rested largely in the hands of the politicians in Sydney, far to the south, and arguably out of touch with their problems.

The ending of convict transportation to the eastern mainland colonies in 1840 had exacerbated the problems of labour shortage for the squatters who hoped to pursue their own policies once separation was gained. Likewise, the merchants of Moreton Bay and the northern parts anticipated greater gains to themselves if they could have a new colony created. During the 1850s all these parties agitated for the creation of a separate colony.

The Colonial Office finally responded to these pressures by establishing in December 1859 the colony of Queensland. This meant creating separate institutions there — a governor and his staff, Parliament, bureaucracy and a judiciary.

Robert Herbert had come to Moreton Bay in late 1859 as both Colonial Secretary for this new colony of Queensland, and as Private

Secretary to its first governor, Sir George Bowen. He had been born in 1831, and educated at Eton and Balliol College, Oxford. He had been, briefly, Private Secretary to the great Liberal Prime Minister, William Gladstone, before resuming legal studies and becoming a barrister. His colonial career was to be spectacular. He not only won, in 1860, a seat in the Legislative Council, but became Queensland's first Premier. As his biographer, Bruce Knox, has noted, this was despite him being —

> young and book-learned, 'a new-chum' and interloper, an
> aristocrat and a careful dresser.

While at Balliol, Herbert had become close friends with John Bramston. The latter had been born in 1832, the son of a politician, and, like his friend, had entered the legal profession, and was admitted to the Bar in 1857. After graduation he shared rooms in London with Herbert. Having shown promise, Bramston's legal future in England seemed assured. Instead, he chose to follow Herbert to Moreton Bay. As Bruce Knox has put it, 'Whatever the process of Herbert's thinking about a colonial excursion, it was somehow shared by his friend: Bramston went to Queensland hard on Herbert's heels'.

In Brisbane Bramston again shared accommodation with Herbert and, as historian Roger Joyce has so nicely put it, 'enjoyed the variety of his [Herbert's] bachelor's life'. Then in December 1860, to quote Knox again —

> the two linked their names and their money to establish the
> estate of 'Herston'. This comprised some 50 acres of well-
> formed land, between Victoria Park and Breakfast Creek,
> some three miles from Brisbane. On it the friends built a
> fine stone house with a wide verandah in the local style.

It became their love and refuge.

There are some clues of their life together in the numerous letters and papers of Herbert's sent to his family in England, especially to his mother. They tell of the establishment of the house and the building up of the property, of their camping trips together and with friends. There is much comment on Bramston, about his rise in colonial politics, his abilities as a horseman and this intriguing passage: 'The Hon John preserves his figure beautifully, and ought to be able to marry when he is at home'.

As to his own bachelor life, Herbert in 1865 wrote to his sister —

> I am certain I could not have got through so many years

hard work but for being a bachelor, and keeping very early hours. The anxieties of a family, and the burden of evening parties may be borne by an idle man, but I really don't think I could have endured them in addition to official work all day.

Although his contemporaries commented upon Herbert's popularity within colonial society, and especially with the ladies, there is never, in his letters, any mention of an attraction to women, or of any intention ever to marry. Yet this would undoubtedly be expected of a man of his class and position.

Good friends, Premier Robert Herbert and John Bramston

In 1863, Bramston followed Herbert into the Legislative Council and served as minister without portfolio until 1866, except for a brief period as Attorney-General in 1865. He does not seem to have been the successful politician that Herbert was.

By 1865 Herbert was beginning to lose his political touch and, as well, 'was weary, and sick and disgruntled with colonial politics'. He yearned for 'another taste of civilisation'. In 1866 he resigned as Premier, and on 20 August sailed for England. Bramston followed some months later.

At this point their careers briefly diverged. Herbert entered the bureaucracy and by 1871 had become Permanent Undersecretary of the Colonial Office. Bramston became the assistant Boundary

Commissioner for Devon and Cornwall. Then, in 1870, he returned to Queensland and for three years again served as Attorney-General. In 1872, at the age of 40, he married, and the following year he returned to England to take up work in the Colonial Office, now headed by Herbert. Bramston died in 1921, having survived by 16 years his friend Herbert, who died unmarried in 1905.

Is this a homosexual love story? While we have to be careful not to project present concepts back into the past — and therefore assume that close same-sex relationships were explicitly 'homo' sexual (a word and concept not invented until 1869 and not in wide currency in English until late in the nineteenth century) — we should also not fall into the opposite trap of denying possible homo-eroticism, or of automatically presuming heterosexuality.

That the friendship between Herbert and Bramston was close, and could perhaps be described as intimate in a broad sense, is undoubted; but there is no evidence one way or another that it had a sexual dimension. This is to be expected. Herbert's letters, in the manner of Victorian correspondence, evidence only a close friendship between him and Bramston. They 'shared lodgings' several times in their lives. In Queensland they went through the experience of creating a new home together, of overcoming the trials and tribulations that this entails.

Herbert's letters home elaborate on the domesticity of their lives together, the shared pleasures, the joy of getting away from the world to be by themselves. If their letters had been written by a man about himself and a female companion, we probably would be in no doubt as to the nature of these lives together, and we would undoubtedly presume a sexual element. But their letters relate to the life of two men together. What should we then presume? A story of ultimately unrequited love? Or of a love that blossomed, and then faced separation for several years, only to flower again later?

Perhaps it doesn't matter what exactly the nature of their relationship was, but since our history so rarely records examples of close male friendships — whatever their nature — it is certainly worthwhile to record this one.

SOURCES: *Australian Dictionary of Biography*, Vols 3 and 4, 1851-1890. 'John Bramston' and 'Robert Herbert' (Melbourne, 1969 & 1972)
Bruce Knox, *The Queensland Years of Robert Herbert, Premier: Letters and Papers* (St Lucia, 1977)

THROWING ON A FROCK

The practice of cross-dressing, or wearing drag, has long had a strong tradition within the homosexual sub-cultures in Australia, especially within 'camp scene' of the 1950s and 1960s. But, in society at large, it is a phenomenon which dates back into the nineteenth century. It is also an area in which we have some of the little documented evidence about women in our history who were transsexual or possibly lesbian transvestites.

The earliest documented instance of cross-dressing that I know of dates from 1835. A male convict, Edmund Carmen, was apprehended in the Wollongong area, south of Sydney, 'dressed in a woman's gown and cape'. He was found guilty of 'Improper Conduct', given fifty lashes and sent back to Sydney, 'not to be assigned again to this District'.

By contrast, the *Sydney Gazette* in 1839 reported a woman being arrested for drunkenness in George Street, Sydney. The authorities were perplexed when they discovered that she was in fact a man in drag. Not knowing what to do, they sobered him up and sent him home.

Then there is the very curious episode involving the Reverend J. J. Westwood. He was a preacher who travelled the countryside in New South Wales, giving sermons, performing funerals, weddings and baptisms. Here is his Journal entry for 3 September 1863 from Deniliquin in the Riverina —

> This evening I was requested by a number of gentlemen at The Wanderer [hotel], to preach them a sermon in the parlour. Declined doing so at the first; but upon being pressed, I replied, 'that if it was for the glory of God, and the good of their souls, I should be happy to do so'.
> After retiring a short time, returned and preached from the following text, in Titus II, 11-13. In the course of my sermon, Mr. Robertson and his servants came in; also a

squatter or cattle dealer, dressed up in woman's clothes. In my text was led to speak faithfully against sin …

I confess I never know just what to make of that episode. Were the hotel habitues sending the preacher up, as seems likely, or was cross-dressing acceptable behaviour in the rural community?

And what are we to make of a member of the Ned Kelly gang of bushrangers, Steve Hart, who frequently rode about in feminine attire? This was probably a disguise to prevent the gang from being recognised from a distance. But Hart seems to have enjoyed it. As part of his Ned Kelly series, Sidney Nolan painted Hart dressed in drag and riding side saddle on the famous occasion when he won a horse race at Greta in Victoria.

There are a number of famous female cross-dressers and in each case the women seem to have been someone we would today class as transsexual.

The strangest case is perhaps that of the jockey Bill Smith. Nothing is known of Bill Smith's early life, but he arrived in North Queensland with two racehorses and established himself as a local identity on country race-courses. He was remembered by old acquaintances as a small figure who was very roughly spoken and given to constant swearing. He added to his reputation for eccentricity by refusing to change with the other jockeys.

As the 1979 *Australian Women's Diary* tells the story —

He won the St Leger Quest in 1902, the Jockey Club Derby in 1903, and the Victoria Oaks in 1909-10.

For the last four years of his life Bill Smith lived near Cairns as a recluse. When he died in 1975 he was found to be a women and was buried as Miss Wilhelmina Smith.

One of the most public women cross-dressers was 'Bill' Edwards. In 1908 she first achieved notoriety when an article was written on her in the radical journal *The Lone Hand*.

Even as recently as 1950, when she was leading a quiet life in a Melbourne suburb, she was not free from the prying eyes of the, inappropriately named, *Truth* newspaper, which reported on her colourful life —

During her travels about the world [she]: Worked as a male clerk and then as a shearer in the outback of Victoria and New South Wales; Took part as a female impersonator entertaining the troops during the Boer War; Obtained the licence of a Melbourne hotel and conducted the business for several years; Owned and trained race horses successfully on Melbourne pony tracks; conducted an S.P. betting business in a lane behind a North Melbourne hotel; ... [and] made several trips around the world as a man. She died a pauper in Melbourne in April 1957.

The most notorious and best know case, however, is that of Eugenia Falleini. She came to Australia as a cabin boy. As Harry Crawford, she twice married. It was much to the consternation of her second wife that she was arrested in 1920 and gaoled for the murder of her first wife some three years before. There was even more consternation when, in gaol, her true gender was discovered. Ah, the days of gender naivety!

Finally, in these days of debate over military discrimination against gays and lesbians, it amazes me that a number of the drag artists from Sydney's clubs in the 1930s ended up, in the 1940s, as soldiers and then as *femme* characters in the army entertainment shows staged by groups such as the Sixth Division Concert Party. Not only that, their skills were highly appreciated by the troops.

The military seem ever ready to accept homosexuals and transvestites when it suits a need, such as for cannon fodder or as entertainers, but are more reluctant to extend equality in employment when that need passes.

SOURCES: Wollongong Historical Society. Wollongong Magistrates Book, 1833-1844. 22 July 1835
Melbourne *Truth*, 7 April 1956
The Lone Hand, 1 January 1908 pp. 304-6
Suzanne Falkiner, *Eugenia — A Man* (Sydney, 1988)
Michael Pate, *An Entertaining War* (Sydney, 1986)

IN FOR A PENNY, IN FOR A POUND!

It is often forgotten that Melbourne was the largest city in Australia from the mid-1850 gold rushes until the first decade of the twentieth century. Indeed, Marvellous Melbourne, as it was known, was one of the largest cities of the British Empire, with close ties to 'mother' England.

As such, it became a point of gravitation for the poor, as well as for the dispossessed younger sons of wealthy families, seeking to make their fortune in the colonies — or escaping from scandal. Such scandal could, of course, include the consequences of being homosexual.

It could be expected, therefore, that Melbourne would be the first city in the country to develop a homosexual sub-culture similar to that which existed in London in the late nineteenth century. Evidence points to this but still remains sketchy.

One interesting piece of evidence which has come to light concerns the existence of one of the institutions of such a sub-culture — a male brothel.

Graham Carberry from the Australian Lesbian and Gay Archives in Melbourne has recently interviewed a gay man, Ken, as part of an oral history program. In the late 1930s, when he was just coming onto the scene, Ken encountered an older homosexual, Harold Stewart, who told him of the existence of such a brothel in suburban Richmond at the turn of the century. Located near the rear of the Town Hall, it was said even to have been patronised by prominent English people, some who moved in Vice-Regal circles, on their visits to the colony of Victoria.

It was apparently owned by a mining engineer who had made money on the goldfields. As to his name and for how long it operated, there is, as yet, no evidence. Much more needs to be researched. In the meantime, we look forward to the eventual publication of the transcripts of the Archives' oral history interviews.

It is against this background that one interesting incident has been documented. It concerns a prostitute who earlier in the century was plying her trade in the Melbourne suburb of Fitzroy.

One of her clients was John McKeeour, a 21-year-old bank clerk who lived in East Collingwood. He had been solicited by her several times on the streets of Fitzroy but had declined to go with her.

In February 1862, he encountered her again outside Myers Bakery. She stopped him and solicited him or, in his terms, 'asked me if I was going to shout'. He, at first, replied that he would not but upon being pressed, consented to go with her.

She took him back to a house in Young Street. There they entered the front room which contained a sofa and which was lit only by a single candle. The candle was blown out. McKeeour thought it all a little strange.

The encounter became even stranger. She lay on the sofa and pulled up her clothes and petticoats. He unbuttoned his trousers and lay on top of her. He then endeavoured to put his hand on her 'private parts', but his hand was firmly pushed away. She took hold of his penis and 'placed it' into her.

It was much to his consternation, and embarrassment, that he was hauled before the courts some eighteen months later to give evidence that he had been induced to have sex with John Wilson, a man!

From the court file, it is obvious that he was shocked to encounter Wilson again, particularly in male attire.

In court, he described how he found the circumstances of the encounter strange. In answer to the questioning of the prosecutor, he stated —

> I penetrated his person and had connection with him — I
> have had connection with females — I did notice a slight
> difference between the connection with the prisoner and
> with females — [the] prisoner's parts seemed colder.

He also admitted that he had paid three shillings and sixpence for the pleasure!

In further evidence to the court, a doctor told of his physical examination of the prisoner, whom he found him to have a 'small penis tied up'.

John McKeeour is the only person on the deposition to give evidence. I do not know if there were others. He, however, was not charged with any offence. John Wilson, though, was found guilty of an unnatural offence and gaoled. We know little more than this about him. Was he acting as an individual? Did he rent the front room of the house in Richmond? Who was the owner of the house, and did the proprietor know what was Wilson's trade? We may well never be able to answer these questions.

When I first wrote this piece I ended the column with the following rather glib comment — 'And is this all just an instance of clever cruising or the earliest evidence we have in Australia of a transsexual encounter?'

Subsequently I have been able to examine the entry on John Wilson in the Prison Register and am not inclined to be so flippant. The awful circumstances of his later life are fully evident.

Wilson is described as being five foot nine inches tall and weighing twelve stone four pounds, with light brown hair, blue eyes and fair complexion when he entered prison. He was thirty-seven years of age. Described as a widower, he had been on Australian soil for three years having been transported from England as a convict.

As if confinement in Pentridge Gaol was not enough, for the first three years of his six year sentence, he was required to wear chains. While generally of 'Good Conduct' he was disciplined on seven separate occasions spending anything from 2 to 20 days in solitary confinement. On 25 July 1896, he died in Pentridge Hospital from a 'disease of the brain and large intestines'.

SOURCES: PROV. Supreme Court. VPRS 264, Capital Case Files. *item*: Queen v John Wilson, 1863 and VPRS 515, Cental Register of Male Prisoners, 1850 -1947. Vol. 10. *item*: John Wilson

CAMPING BY A BILLABONG

The homo-social, and even the homo-erotic or homosexual, nature of Australian 'mateship', particularly in rural areas, has long been speculated upon. Russell Ward, in what now seems a rather coy statement, acknowledged in 1958 in his *The Australian Legend* that —

the bushman, blessedly ignorant of psychological theory, appeased ... [a] spiritual hunger by a sublimated homosexual relationship with a mate, or a number of mates, of his own sex.

Ward also believed that, for the majority of men, the 'quite unconscious sublimation' would not have occurred if there had been women around. In this he is no doubt correct yet, nonetheless, it is difficult to believe that there was no sex at all or that no genuine 'homosexual' relationships developed.

As noted earlier, Bishop Ullathore told the Molesworth Committee of his belief that same-sex activity was common among stockmen in country districts. There is, however, little in the way of detail from court records, which predominantly recorded events in urban areas. Up country, people were generally free from prying eyes. Sometimes a certain naivety was exhibited, or even a blind eye turned, towards couples known to be 'mates'.

Sometimes, however, people did get caught. Robert Connell was one. He was a shepherd on a property at Kyneton, Victoria in 1862. He shared an outroom with Charles Bourbon, who obviously took his fancy. One evening, as Bourbon tells it —

I made my bed — I took off my clothes and the prisoner was about to come into my bed. I said to him, "Make your own bed." — he did so — as the prisoner was undressing he said to me "should I give you a f — — —."

Bourbon declined the offer and went to sleep only to awake 'an hour before daybreak by feeling the prisoner in my person'.

In 1873, Thomas King and Herman Bishop, two workers on the Glen Swan Estate on the Hastings River, Port Macquarie were convicted of attempted sodomy. A fellow worker, Tom Garside, had come upon them in the barracks —

> I heard voices in the hut. I recognised the voice of the prisoner Thos King and Prisoner [Herman] Bishop. I heard King say to Bishop –
> "Come here you won't get another chance."
> Bishop replied, "I am sleepy."
> King said, "I'll come into you."

Garside burst in upon them and —

> saw the prisoner King and Bishop on a bed with only their shirts on — Bishop was lying partly on his stomach and side — King was on top of Bishop or partly on his side ... I saw that King was withdrawing his penis from Bishop's fundament ... their parts were fully exposed to me ... King's penis was standing at the time — or in a state of erection.

Bishop panicked at being discovered. He pleaded with Garside not to tell what he had seen, since —

> It's all King's fault for he told me he was a 'Morpherodite' [sic] and a ... power had come over him and for me to come into his room and satisfy him.

Bishop then gave one of the most novel excuses I have yet come across for having homosexual sex — 'He said he did it for the progress of science'.

From time to time I hear stories from older gay men of couples who were shearers or itinerant workers and who roamed the countryside earlier this century. But sometimes young single men wandering on their own may have been the object of desire for other swagmen. Clive Moore has recently brought to my attention a comment by William (Billy) Hughes (Prime Minister of Australia from 1915 to 1923) who in the mid-1880s carried his swag around Queensland —

> Hughes was small in stature and quite prudish, according to one of his biographers, Malcolm Booker, seldom discussing sex. Yet in old age he admitted that 'one of his greatest worries when camping alone in the bush was that he would be subjected to a homosexual attack by another wayfarer'.

While this probably says more about Hughes' attitude to sexual matters, it is an interesting observation nonetheless.

Another rural episode case occurred in South Australia in 1915. Two men were caught fucking in a room off the bar of the Tarcoola Hotel. Both worked on the construction of the East-West railway — one was a 27-year-old labourer called Scotty; the other, a 36-year-old Norwegian called The Foreigner, was the local Australian Workers Union representative. They had been spied earlier drunkenly embracing in a corner of the bar.

Both were found guilty 'for an unsavoury act'. Interestingly, both were given a three year sentence. Normally, The Foreigner, as the 'passive' partner, would have been treated as an accessory but in this case the judge gave him the same sentence 'because of his influence over the accused'.

From the evidence, one cannot be conclusive about the sexuality of Scotty but not so in the case of The Foreigner. Three years later, after his release, he was again convicted for attempted buggery and given another two year sentence.

With the Depression of the 1930s many took to the road in country areas looking for work. An insight into the lives of the men who roamed in groups is given by Frank Huelin in his autobiographical account *Keep Moving* —

> The trend was for grouping — five or six banding together
> for their mutual benefit and protection ... [but] ... alliances
> were made and broken as the norms of social and sexual
> morality cracked under the stress of this nomadic existence.
> In this society such things as metho-drinking, petty theft —
> from outside our ranks — and sexual perversion were
> accepted as inevitable.

He later goes on to illustrate the homosexual aspect of this vagabondage with the story of a pair who had joined his group. After a spot of trouble with the railway police, the group had been thrown off a freight train near Broken Hill —

> The pair who had travelled with us preferred to continue
> on their own. They filled their billies and headed off along
> a barely discernible track which led away from the railway
> in the direction of the distant iron roof.
> We tried to persuade them against chancing their arm in
> what was virtually semi-desert country but they were
> confident they could make it without any trouble.
> We had a strong suspicion about the relationship which

existed between them — the older man claimed the younger as his nephew and they may have been so, but we concluded there was a more intimate sexual relationship — that the younger was the older man's 'bimbo', and that this was the principle reason for their go-it-alone attitude.

SOURCES: PROV. Supreme Court. VRPS 264, Capital Case Files. *item*: Queen v Robert Connell, 1863
AONSW. Central Criminal Court. Depositions. 9/6560, 16 April 1873
SRSA. GRG 36/1, Box 83, July 1915
Clive Moore, 'The Frontier Makes Strange Bedfellows: Masculinity, Mateship and Homosexuality in Colonial Queensland'. A paper delivered to the Australian Centre for Gay and Lesbian Research, University of Sydney. 6 August 1993
Frank Huelin, *Keep Moving* (Sydney, 1973) pp. 48, 139-40
Russell Ward, *The Australian Legend* (Melbourne, 1958) pp. 99-100

THE OSCAR WILDES OF SYDNEY

We know that Australian cities had thriving homosexual sub-cultures by the 1920s, but when did these first develop? It is impossible to be precise, but there is certainly evidence that these can be dated back to at least the last decade of the nineteenth century.

The earliest reference we have to a homosexual 'group' comes from the diary of William Chidley, an outspoken sex reformer of the early twentieth century. As a young man in Adelaide in 1888, he came across several other young men who mixed in theatrical circles —

> They were fond of performing and singing at amateur
> minstrel shows and had developed a certain comic vein
> they thought original, though it reminded me of
> professional corner-men. However I enjoyed their singing
> and drinking and went to their lodgings several nights to
> play cards.
> One night they asked me to stay all night, and on going to a
> room with two beds I was told to have one. Presently one
> of the young men came in and commenced to undress.
> Before going to his bed he made a remark which, though I
> had been drinking, opened my eyes. I told him to shut up
> and go to bed.

If young men had found each other's company in the provincial city of Adelaide, what was happening in the larger cities of Melbourne and Sydney?

With regard to Sydney, one exciting piece of evidence was uncovered in 1993 by historian Garry Wotherspoon. A little known Sydney scandal sheet, *The Scorpion*, followed up its report on the Oscar Wilde trial in London in 1895 with an article entitled, 'The Oscar Wilde's [sic] of Sydney'. Among its claims were that —

> The state of things in London as regards this horrible vice is
> also the condition of affairs in Sydney. It is idle for people
> to shut their eyes to this fact. It has been planted here by

the English exiles. The men who escaped the
Cleveland-street prosecution found shelter in Australia, and
there are many of them at present in Sydney.

The 'Cleveland-street prosecution' is a reference to a celebrated
raid on a London homosexual brothel in 1889. The article goes on to
claim that —

Many of the leading hotels and billiard saloons are haunted
by these characters, whose presence is advertised by
effeminate style of speech, and the adoption of the names
of celebrated actresses.

More importantly, the article continues, 'A haunt is said to exist in
Bourke Street, Surry Hills and that part of College-street from
Boomerang-street to Park-street is a parade for them.'

Today Bourke Street is near the centre of Sydney's so called 'gay
ghetto' with its bars and clubs. Just what was the nature of the
nineteenth century 'haunt' — a bar, brothel or boarding house
perhaps — is yet to be determined. However, we have long suspected
that the stretch of College Street beside Hyde Park existed as a beat
back into last century. Here now is the evidence.

Sydney at the time was a town of four hundred thousand people
most of whom lived within a five kilometres radius of the General
Post Office. Melbourne, the 'second city of the Empire', was almost
one third larger in population. In the 1890s, both had thriving
theatrical sub-cultures and literary circles that passed for a bohemian
sub-culture.

In Melbourne, we know that the poet Bernard O'Dowd was a
correspondent of Walt Whitman, whom he referred to as 'My dear
master'. Like Whitman, he was a devotee of the concept of the 'dear
love of Comrades' — the extolling of the virtues of comradeship
among working men. While this is the espousal of homo-social
behaviour, nonetheless the evidence points to a homo-erotic element
in it as well.

The circle of artists and writers in Sydney was a lively one. A
number of the writers in this circle, such as the poets Francis Adams
and John Le Gay Brereton (whose poetry today appears in gay
anthologies), shared O'Dowd's fascination with the 'love of
comrades'. The circle was quite diverse and included well known 'life
long bachelors', such as David Scott Mitchell, later to give his name
to the Australiana collection in the State Library of New South
Wales.

We cannot yet be sure about the sexual orientation of any of the adherents of this circle but there was one important person who was friendly with many members of this group and who was homosexual — the Governor of New South Wales, Earl Beauchamp.

EARL, BEAUCHAMP.
Governor New South Wales, 1899-1900.

As a bachelor, he had taken up residence at Government House in 1898. He was interested in literary and artistic matters and established contact with the bohemian circle, much to the chagrin of Sydney's elite society. He also was generous in his patronage — for instance, paying for the visit to England of the writer Henry Lawson.

Beauchamp returned to England in 1900. We know that he had a fondness for Sydney, returning to visit on many occasions. He also had an admiration for the men of Sydney. In 1931 he wrote —

> The men are splendid athletes, like the greek statues. Their skins are tanned by sun and wind, and I doubt whether anywhere in the world are finer specimens of manhood than in Sydney. The lifesavers at the bathing beaches are wonderful.

In England Beauchamp married. In 1935, however, his wife threatened to institute divorce proceedings on the grounds of his homosexuality. This caused a major scandal in London. In response to this, King George V made his infamous remark, 'I thought men like that shot themselves!'

SOURCES: Susan McInerny (ed), *The Diaries of William Chidley* (St Lucia, 1977), pp. 87-88

The Scorpion, 24 April 1895, p. 2

Australian Dictionary of Biography Vol. 7, 1890-1930 'Earl Beauchamp' (Melbourne, 1979)

Sydney Morning Herald, 2 March 1931, p. 9

INTO THE WOODS

Historically, beats often provided the first opportunity for the men whom we now call homosexual to meet. Few people, however, realise that the history of some beats in the Australian cities of Melbourne, Brisbane, Adelaide and Sydney seem to go back to the nineteenth century. Take, as an example, the Hyde Park/Domain area in Sydney.

In earlier years the area was larger and more heavily wooded than now. As early as 1830, it had a reputation as a (hetero-) sexual playground. Indeed, as the *Sydney Gazette* complained in March of that year, 'The Domain is becoming a resort for very unproper characters of both sexes'. The paper called for regular police patrols.

The first incident I know of men being caught fucking in Hyde Park was in 1882. Late one night in May, James Teece and Louis

Louis Calonize and the very wet James Teece

47

Calonize were apprehended under some bushes. The response of James Teece to the constables, while amusing, nonetheless provided evidence for the conviction of both men —

> Don't do anything Sir and I'll tell you the Truth. This man
> (referring to Calonize) took my trousers down, put his
> thing in my behind and made me all wet.

Calonize, as the active partner, received eight years' hard labour, Teece got three. How often in our history have people convicted themselves in a similar manner by blurting it all to the police?

The date of this incident may indicate that the beat on the College Street side of the park may have an even older history than the 1890s.

Evidence would suggest that police began to patrol Hyde Park regularly, seeking out 'perverts', sometime just after the First World War. Herbert Moran reports that in 1935 two vice squad officers were responsible for the arrest of one hundred and fifty men over a period of two years and that most of these arrests were the result of the police acting 'as a decoy'. In the words of another commentator, they found these assignments 'most distasteful'.

In the early 1920s, the New South Wales Attorney-General received complaints from several prominent citizens about police harassment in the Park. (Some of them, it seems, had been arrested and charged with indecency but, cleverly, had avoided public disgrace by using false names.) Their complaints led to an interesting encounter as described in Vince Kelly's biography of an undercover policeman, Frank Fahey, called *The Shadow*.

The Attorney-General had expressed his concern about police activity in the Park. The police, in turn, invited him to come and investigate for himself. He agreed, and on the chosen evening accompanied the police to keep watch on the College Street lavatory which since has been demolished. Fahey's biographer takes up the story —

> That evening he waited in the shadow of the trees in the
> park and watched with the detective-sergeant the men who
> went in and out. [At the police suggestion] the minister left
> him and entered the lavatory ... It was only a few minutes
> later that the Attorney-General and another man walked
> out of the lavatory together and entered the park. The man
> with the Attorney-General was stroking the Minister's face
> and inviting him softly to go further into the Park.

As they approached, the police leapt out and made a grab at the
man with the Minister but he, nonetheless, escaped —
   The Attorney-General was both amused and reproachful.
   He said, "Damn it, sergeant, you were too impetuous! If
   you had only waited a minute you could have grabbed one
   of those perverts. There was another one in there, too.
   Heaven's I would never have believed it!"
A police officer, however, had to explain that —
   the man who got away was no pervert, Sir. But he thought
   you were one. If I hadn't been here he would have bashed
   you in another second or two and robbed you.
There were poofter bashers back then as well as now.

One of the pleasures of Hyde Park, detail of the Archibald Fountain

In the 1930s, the new Archibald Fountain, with its butch male
statues (and a hint of S&M?) was, apparently, the homosexual
'meeting-place' in the Park, as is described by Kylie Tennant in her
novel *Tell Morning This*.
   She has a group of men invade a meeting to protest at what they
wrongly understand is an attempt to have the fountain removed from

the Park. When alerted to their mistake, the 'little group of art lovers', as she has them term themselves, apologises and withdraws.

After the Second World War, the beat still extended from the Archibald Fountain down to and along the College Street side of the Park where, as we have seen, it had existed from the late nineteenth century. According to Sydney gay activist Lex Watson, in 1956 the footpath on College Street was narrowed (and remains so) in order to eradicate homosexuals from Sydney. (A fine piece of lateral thinking by the Council and we all know how successful it was!) Unfortunately the appropriate file at the City Council, which could tell us more on the reasoning for this, no longer exists.

Sometimes the beat extended across into Hyde Park South. Robert Connell explains why —

> There were times when it would venture across Park Street to the place where [the] Captain Cook statue stands. It always seemed quite innocuous from the front, but many of us found the wrong angle from the side, in which the telescope seemed to become a giant erection and he was masturbating. It seemed to us that this was a gigantic joke the sculptor had played on the city when it was created in the Victorian era.

In the 1960s, the beat moved across College Street and into Boomerang Street, running down to William Street. It is from this beat that the social club called The Boomerangs, formed in 1967, took its name. The group, one of the oldest continuing gay and lesbian social groups in Sydney, celebrated its twenty-fifth anniversary in May 1992.

By the early 1970s, the increasing attractions of Kings Cross with its new bars, and then Oxford Street with its gay venues, saw the decline of Hyde Park as an active beat.

SOURCES: AONSW. Central Criminal Court. Depositions. item: 4/6679
Herbert Moran, *Viewless Winds* (London, 1939) p. 233
Vince Kelly, *The Shadow* (Sydney, 1954) Ch. 6
Kylie Tennant, *Tell Morning This* (Sydney, 1963) pp. 226-7
Robert Connell, 'The Way it Was: Recollections of the Gay Scene in Sydney' *Oxford Weekender News* 20 October 1983

"Just For Fun"

Described by His Honour as 'a pest to Society', Edward
Cahill, a young man, was sentenced to seven years'
imprisonment with hard labour for an unnatural offence.

This brief quote from *The West Australian* newspaper of 1909 gives
little indication of the importance of this case, and of Edward Cahill,
in the gay history of Perth, and indeed of the rest of Australia.

Quite simply, Edward Cahill, who had a prior conviction for wife
desertion, is perhaps one of the first people we can identify from
official records as a self-acknowledged homosexual.

On the night of 16 November 1909, Police Constable James
Lightly was on duty in the inner suburb of North Perth. As he
patrolled through Russell Square at 11.30 pm he saw 'a heap on the
grass about twenty yards from the path'. (It was common for street
lighting to be turned out at mid-evening.) Lightly moved toward the
'heap' for a closer look. In his own words, 'I noticed the heap roll
apart and I noticed that it was two men'. He enquired what they were
doing. The other man with Cahill, never to be identified, replied that
they 'were just having a lay down'. It now seems incredible to us, and
is surely a reflection of the naivety of the times, that the constable
told them to be on their way, and himself continued his patrol
through the Park.

Unfortunately for Cahill, after five or six yards, Lightly looked
around and saw him 'trying to pull his trousers up'. He ran back and
as he did so the two men started to make off in the other direction.
The other man escaped, though not before falling over a small fence
bordering the footpath within the Park. Lightly overtook Cahill, who
also was running away but with some difficulty as his trousers were
unbuttoned, 'his braces undone and his shirt shoved in in a hurry'.

Cahill at first tried to get out of the predicament he now was so
clearly in by stating, 'I was lying on the grass and the man came up

to me and started to feel me up and wanted to stuff me.' He then pleaded with Lightly not to take him in 'for the sake of his Mother and Sister', but to no avail.

At the Police Station, however, faced with the inevitable, he not only changed his attitude but he seems to have become quite brazen about his activities (rather stupidly, it must be said, for he ends up convicting himself). After being charged, and while on the way to be examined at Perth Hospital, he freely said to another Constable, 'I'll own up to the man having connection with me.' And when the astonished Constable replied, 'This is a funny game,' and then asked him, 'Why did he do it?' Cahill boldly replied, 'Just for fun.' He also added (perhaps boasted?), 'It's not the first time it's been done to me. It's been done to me several times before.'

Later, a doctor who had physically examined his anus and 'found the appearance consistent with an unnatural offence having been

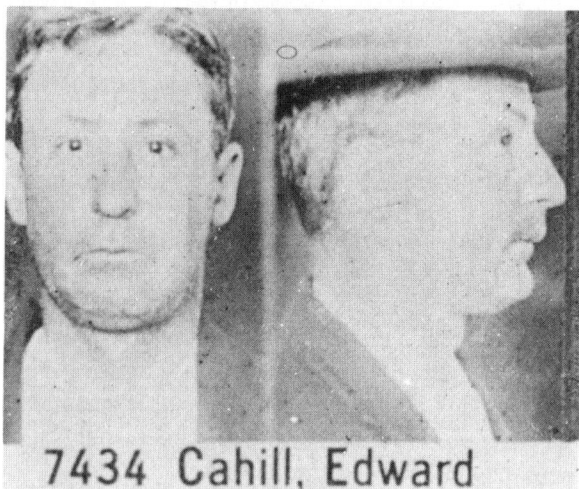

7434 Cahill, Edward

recently committed', though, of course, one wonders about this and other 'expert' medical evidence. (It should be remembered that for years it was an accepted 'fact' by doctors that homosexuals all were born with a funnel-shaped anus!) In any case, Cahill freely stated (without shame?) to the doctor that 'he had practised the vice for over two years.'

The case is important not only because of Edward Cahill himself and what happened to him, but because it hints at the existence in Perth of a beat culture. This in itself raises questions as to the possibility of an emerging homosexual sub-culture in Perth at the time. As yet, however, there is not enough evidence to be conclusive on these points.

But the case also is memorable for another reason. When arrested, Cahill had in his possession a pot of Vaseline, which was presented as evidence in Court. It is the only instance I know which documents so early the use of Vaseline as a lubricant. Interestingly, three years later a receipt from a Fremantle chemist for a three penny jar of Vaseline was used as evidence in another case in the Perth Supreme Court.

Russell Square is bordered on one side by James Street where today a number of Perth's gay bars are located. In the remote past it would seem to have been a beat and in the recent past it has been a commercial beat for prostitutes. It is now the place where Perth's gay and lesbian marches usually begin and end. We now have another reason to consider it an important site. Maybe the Perth community should consider establishing a fitting memorial. Perhaps a statue of Edward Cahill — holding erect a jar of Vaseline of course!

SOURCES: *The West Australian,* 8 December 1909, p.4
SAWA. Supreme Court. WAS 122, Criminal Files 1830 — . *item*: 4170, Edward Cahill, 1909

A FIRST CLASS BOY

Poor William Amy. He didn't stand much of a chance really. After all, the good name of the newly formed Royal Australian Navy was at stake.

In 1913, following the federation of the Australian colonies in 1901, the RAN became independent from the British Royal Navy, much to the chagrin of the Sea Lords in London. Nonetheless, the new navy seems still to have carried on the fine British tradition of 'Rum, Sodomy and the Lash', as Churchill later was to describe it.

In that year, also, on St Valentine's Day, and at the age of 14 years, William Henry Amy, of Port Melbourne, volunteered for 7 years' service as a naval rating and was assigned to HMAS *Tirgira*. His Certificate of Service describes him as being small, at four foot nine and a half inches, with dark hair, bluish eyes and a medium complexion, and with no apparent wounds or scars.

By 14 November 1913, he was transferred to HMAS *Melbourne* and had been promoted to the rank of Boy 1st Class. Now that he really seems to have been! Within six months, on 11 June 1914, he was before a court-martial, having contracted syphilis up the bum.

He had gone to the sick bay on 12 May, complaining of haemorrhoids. After examination, the ship's surgeon, William Carr, came to the opinion that Amy was suffering from something far more serious. His diagnosis was subsequently confirmed by two other doctors who specialised in treating venereal disease. One was even prepared to go so far as to state in court that, in his opinion, 'this sore could only have been caused by contact with an infected male organ.'

The court, however, chose not to pursue this evidence too closely even when it turned its attention to the possible circumstances in which Amy could have become infected.

Evidence was heard from Petty Officer Frank Taylor, who had overall charge of the boys on the ship. He admitted to the court that he had warned all the boys 'about skylarking about with the men, and [if] at any time they were interfered with by any person, they were to report to me at once'.

The court, again, never pursued what, to us, is the obvious question. Why had Taylor felt the need to issue such counsel in the first place? Was it generally understood, but never publicly admitted, that in the navy there would be attempts by seamen to have sex with the boys?

With regard to Amy in particular, Taylor said that he had seen people skylarking with him and that 'I pointed out to him that he had no business to skylark with the men, and pointed out to him the danger in doing so'.

He was never asked what he meant by 'danger'. When asked, however, what he meant by 'skylarking' the following exchange took place —

Well sir, pulling them about.

Wrestling with them?

Yes sir, you could call it wrestling.

One member of the court was immediately concerned that this was being done in 'an indecent manner'. Taylor was quick to reassure, 'No sir, they were wrestling with them in the ordinary way as two persons would skylark together'.

Maddeningly for us, having settled the question as to the proper manner of the behaviour of the seamen, this line of questioning was stopped. One wonders if it was all getting a little too close to the truth? And what did Taylor mean by 'ordinary'? These questions are answerable only by speculation.

Earlier, the court had concerned itself with the circumstances which had led Taylor to feel the need to caution Amy. It seems that Amy liked to be often in the company of the older men on the ship. Indeed the caution had related to a specific incident when Amy had slept on the upper deck, on a humid night during coal loading, with the older sailors rather than down on the mess deck with the other boys. This, apparently, was not the first time he had done so.

It would seem probable to assume from the evidence that it was there, on the upper deck, that he became infected but this matter also was not pursued by the court.

The court found him 'guilty of uncleanliness, whereby he, the said William Henry Amy, became infected with syphilis *in ano*'. He was sentenced to twenty-six months' imprisonment and then to be 'dismissed with disgrace'.

The whole case was treated as if in isolation. No further investigation took place to ascertain how Amy might have become infected nor to find the person who was responsible. No other person was charged. The reason is obvious. After all, the navy could hardly undertake an inquiry which might publicly reveal that sodomy was practised in its ranks.

William Amy may or may not have been homosexual. In retrospect, it seems his real misfortune was in having to explore his sexuality in the very wrong place (or was it, given the implications of other evidence, the right place?) and to have been unlucky enough to have been caught out and to have got the clap!

SOURCE: AA (ACT). Dept of Defence, CRS A471, Court Martial files, 1911 — .
item: 103, William Henry Amy

Wynyard Square with Carrington Street on the left

THE QUEER HOUSE

One of the most fascinating episodes from our history is that of the Queer House.

During the First World War, the attention of Sydney police was alerted to the comings and goings of residents in a house located in Carrington Street, Wynard Square. A woman from a neighbouring house had complained to the police that the supposedly respectable young men lodging in the house next door appeared to be holding several young women captive during the day. It seemed that these women were only allowed to go out during the evening in the company of the men.

The police sent undercover constable Joe Chuck (believe me!) to investigate. He called at the house on the pretence of looking for lodgings. Vince Kelly, Chuck's biographer, takes up the story —

> The door was opened by a good-looking young woman dressed in a Japanese kimono. Chuck noticed that she wore a wedding ring and an engagement ring with three large diamonds. Her smile was pleasant, and her voice deep and throaty.
>
> She replied to his inquiry that 'We only take in persons who are personally known to my husband and me, or to some of our friends in the house'.

Chuck persisted with his request for accommodation but, seeing he was getting nowhere, he departed and proceeded to interview the neighbour who had made the complaint. From her answers, he became deeply suspicious.

Several days later he returned in police uniform pretending to be checking the electoral roll for the forthcoming conscription referendum. (This dates the episode to just before either October 1916 or December 1917, when the two referenda were held). He checked with the young woman the names of the men living in the house and these were given. When he asked for the names of the young women, she became flustered and refused to supply any. It was then that —

> Chuck realised with a shock that the 'woman' was possibly not a woman at all, but a pervert dressed in woman's clothes, yet looking so much the part of the well groomed, respectable housewife that he hesitated to believe she could be anything else.

He decided to proceed warily. He returned to the police station where, as Kelly says —

> His story was received at first with incredulity. A house filled entirely with sexual perverts, who were, in every other respect, *living normally and honestly* [my emphasis], posed a problem without precedent.

Chuck was instructed to keep the Queer House under observation. Two nights later, he and two constables were waiting in the Square when they saw three young men leave the house. The police followed them —

> They met in George Street another man who was like themselves, nattily dressed, but who was undeniably wearing lipstick and whose face was rouged. They divided into couples and embraced affectionately. Chuck and his colleagues moved in and arrested the four of them for offensive behaviour.

Kelly continues the story. 'Their prisoners gave no trouble. At the police station, when searched, their pockets contained women's toilet accessories, and two of them wore women's silk underwear'. They listened, with a 'sense of disgust', as their prisoners told *'without shame'* [my emphasis] of life within the house — how the six men lived as three couples; how the 'wife' of the lessee — the one who had answered the door to Chuck — was known as 'Mother Superior' and how 'her word was law' in the house. They also talked about their circle of homosexual friends, which included at least one lesbian.

The police had also seized from the house a large cache of photographs and letters which 'contained some extraordinary love passages which the perverts had written to each other'.

These letters would be a wonderful source for the history of the emerging homosexual sub-culture in Sydney in the period before and during the war, but they do not seem to have survived. Indeed, so far, I have been unable even to find a file on the case. This has puzzled me for some years though in recently re-reading Kelly's biography I think I now know why.

He states that the four men were charged only with offensive behaviour. If this was so then no criminal file would have been created. And if this is the case, the residents of the Queer House could probably count themselves as fortunate. In later years, the police would have questioned them endlessly, gained admissions of buggery, which then would have resulted in them being sent to prison for several years. The only other consequence of the case, according to Kelly, was that all six were forced to vacate the house.

Even so, it makes me angry that this occurred to people whom all admit were living so normally and honestly. They do seem to be gutsy young men but, while I am pleased that they got off so lightly, at the same time I feel frustrated that they were not charged and that consequently no file exists. This is a historian's dilemma. I'd just love to read those letters!

SOURCE: Vince Kelly, *The Bogeyman: The career of Sgt Joe Chuck* (Sydney, 1956)

POUNDING THE BEAT

Some of Sydney's better known beats of today have a history that goes back to at least the inter-war period when the city was expanding beyond its nineteenth century boundaries. And as one might expect, the incidence of police harassment similarly has a long history.

Some of the most frequented beats are in several of Sydney's now more respectable suburbs. Take, for example, St Leonards Park on the lower North Shore of Sydney. Donald (40), a fitter from Enfield, and Phillip (21), a playwright from Camperdown, were arrested there in October 1934. Phillip was sucking Donald off when the regular police patrol apprehended them. Phillip defended his actions, telling the police, 'I can't help being a pervert.'

Both pleaded guilty and received a sentence of one year's hard labour. One aspect of their case that is interesting is that both probably crossed the Harbour Bridge, opened only two years before, in order to get to the park. I suspect this illustrates one aspect of the history of the beat culture in Australia. In order to 'do the beat' people often did travel, sometimes for miles away from their own suburb.

Some stories are tragic.

In November 1931, John Kirkpatrick was charged with indecently assaulting Robert Hodgson but the charges were dropped. Intriguingly, some weeks later the same Robert Hodgson was in turn charged but this time with indecently assaulting John Kirkpatrick.

What went wrong? Was one man forced to give evidence against the other? Unfortunately we will probably never know, for, on 9 December, the New South Wales *Police Gazette* records that Robert Hodgsdon (45) was 'Committed for trial at the Quarter Sessions, but has since committed suicide.'

Within the city itself the well-known beats at various city underground railway stations, at the toilet (since demolished) in

Regent Street near the Mortuary Station, and at the Domain Baths all operated from at least the 1920s. All were subject at different times to police surveillance which led to numerous arrests.

Probably the best known beat within the city, after Hyde Park, was Lang Park in Grosvenor Street. Many people were arrested here by zealous police, even people who were not engaged in any homosexual activity at all. As we shall see in a later chapter, often they were induced to plead guilty in the hope that the case would be quietly dealt with by the courts and that they would avoid any scandal.

Interestingly, those who were prepared to challenge the police in court sometimes got off. Well, they may have done that too but what I mean is they had their cases dismissed! An important lesson.

One of the most heart-rending stories occurred in 1938. Police were mounting regular patrols of the toilets in the changing room at Petersham Oval, still a well known beat. On the evening of 14 January, they went to 'a locker room at the rear of the grandstand'. Two policemen 'climbed to a manhole in the ceiling' while the other two 'remained on the floor and near the door of the dressing room'.

At 8.30, they observed the arrival of a young man, a 19-year-old apprentice wood mechanist whom I will refer to as 'Bernard' as he may still be alive. Constable Thomas King gave evidence that Bernard 'selected a bay of the urinal a compartment immediately below us. I saw him take his penus [sic] out. It was in a full state of erection'.

A little later Felix, a 32-year-old tailor, entered the lavatory. and made conversation with Bernard whose —

> penus [sic] was still in his hand in a state of erection and
> he was rubbing it up and down ... I saw [Felix] place his
> hand around [Bernard's] penus [sic] and catch hold of it. I
> then saw [Felix] bend his head until it was in line with his
> own hand ... [Felix's] mouth was close to his own hand ... I
> saw [Felix's] head move several times in a back and
> forward motion.

Despite their vantage point above, the police had their vision of the scene obscured and were unable to see all that was going on. Nonetheless, having a pretty good idea, they swooped and made their arrests.

On the way to the police station Bernard somehow managed to escape. Unfortunately for him, he was known to one of the policemen. After midnight, Detective Sergeant Williams went to the family home. There he had a conversation with Bernard's parents and at 12.20 am his father went to the sleep-out and brought Bernard to the dining room.

On his arrival his mother asked, according to the policemen's testimony —

> What has happened son? Bernard cried and put his arms around his mother's neck and said I can't tell you Mum.
> I said to Bernard, Do you remember me? He said yes.
> I said I have explained to your parents the nature of your conduct in the lavatory. I am going to take you to Petersham Police Station where you will be charged.

Felix pleaded guilty and received twelve months' hard labour. Bernard pleaded guilty to aiding in an indecent assault and, despite evidence that this was not the first occasion on which he had frequented that beat, he received a three year good behaviour bond.

Bernard may be considered to be lucky. Or was he? What happened to his apprenticeship as a result of the conviction? And what of his future life? Did word spread about the conviction? Was he barred from military service in the war years because of it?

These questions I can't yet answer, but the story leaves me with a great deal of anger towards the police and the politicians who, because of their laws and their enforcement of them, ruined many a life.

SOURCE: AONSW. Sydney Quarter Sessions — Depositions. *item*: 10/3843
1 February 1938 (No. 76)

KING OF THE WEST END

The 1930s saw the arrest and gaoling of two important political figures from two different Australian cities — Aubrey Maddocks in Sydney and Albert Edwards in Adelaide. Both arrests took place as a result of the use of police informers.

Sydney Aubrey Maddocks, a successful New South Wales State public servant, had made enemies on his rise to the top. From 1930, he had been head of the Police Department, where apparently he had clashed with senior police, before being appointed by the newly elected conservative government in 1932, to the position of Commissioner for Transport. The appointment was resented by senior bureaucrats within the Commission, who subsequently took every opportunity to undermine his position.

Five years later, no doubt to the delight of his enemies, Maddocks' career and family life lay in ruins as he stood in the dock of Darlinghurst Court to be sentenced to eighteen months' imprisonment for indecently assaulting 17-year-old Mikiel John Adams and committing an unnatural act with him.

Maddocks had met Adams, whom he knew under another name, through a chance encounter in November 1936. It would seem that Adams had mixed in shady circles since his early teens. In court, the police stated that 'the boy was definitely a pervert from the age of 12 or 14 years'.

He may even have been a prostitute. In any case, Maddocks became increasingly friendly with him, often seeing him on his own. These moments proved a respite from the bureaucratic hassles of his everyday life.

Adams was not above exploiting this 'friendship', demanding money from Maddocks and even stealing from him. That Maddocks was prepared to put up with this leads one to the suspicion that the relationship between them was sexual from early on.

On 1 March 1937, Adams contacted Maddocks and arranged a

meeting at which he said he would return certain items he had stolen. After a meal, Maddocks drove with Adams to Lane Cove National Park. It was there that the police found them naked in the car.

There is no doubt that Maddocks, for whatever reason, had been led into a trap. In court, Adams admitted that the police had dropped him at the point where he had arranged to meet Maddocks and that he had arranged with them for Maddocks to be caught.

Adams was not charged with any offence because of his relationship with the police. Presumably they had something on him in order to gain his co-operation in the first place but for how long he had been working with them I do not know.

Maddocks served out his sentence, with remission for good behaviour, at Bathurst Gaol. He was last heard of as a petrol station proprietor on the North Coast of New South Wales.

Even more publicised was the arrest and trial in 1931 of the South Australian parliamentarian Albert (Bert) Edwards, on charges of committing both an unnatural offence and an act of gross indecency.

Edwards was a successful hotel keeper and State Labor politician in the 'West End' of the city of Adelaide. He was a prominent and important local identity. His personal style was somewhat 'florid' as Susan Edgar illustrates —

> Off-white suits, homburg hat, bowtie and suede shoes
> (suede shoes were supposed to indicate effeminacy in
> South Australia then). The effect was loud and snazzy,
> especially for Adelaide, but Bert was always fastidiously
> groomed.

No matter, he was popularly seen as a champion of the poor. To his supporters he was known as 'the king of the West End'.

Edwards, however, had made enemies both within the conservative Adelaide establishment as well as in the hierarchy of his own party. According to Susan Edgar, his opponents referred to him as a 'Tammany Hall boss'.

It is against this background that the circumstances of his arrest must be seen. Here also there is strong evidence to suggest that the police were actively involved in constructing the evidence to be used against Edwards — he had been pursuing in State Parliament the issue of a fatal shooting in which a policeman was involved.

The main witness against Edwards was a 17-year-old criminal,

John Mundy. John had been a male prostitute and was currently serving time for indecent assault. He was also an ex-employee of Edwards. In court, he did admit that he hoped to get a shortened sentence by giving evidence against Edwards. Edwards was convicted and sentenced to five years' hard labour.

Many of Edwards' supporters and political colleagues believed that Bert had been framed by the police (in a sense he had) and the Adelaide establishment. Despite the scandalous nature of the charges

Bert Edwards, hotelier, politician, sporting patron

against him, they saw him as a working-class martyr and remained loyal to him throughout his period in prison.

After his release, Edwards went back to his old occupation of hotel keeper. He remained a constant critic of the police and ten years later they again brought similar charges against him. In this case he was lucky. The two witnesses so tripped up on their stories that the case against him was dismissed.

Edwards remained a very popular identity. In 1948 he won back a seat on the Adelaide City Council, much to the chagrin of the 'respectable' burghers of Adelaide. He held the seat until his death some fifteen years later.

In his will he left money not only to a range of charities, but as a long time supporter of the West Adelaide Football Club, he left money for the construction of 'a footballers training room'!

Presumably his ghost haunts it still.

SOURCES: Donald King, 'Transport Commissioner Railroaded' *Campaign* No. 42
    (April 1979), p. 11
Australian Dictionary of Biography Vol. 8. 1890-1939 'Albert Edwards' (Melbourne,
    1981)
Susan Edgar, 'The King of the West End' *National Times* 2 May 1982, pp. 12-15

A HORRIBLE WOMAN,
A DISGUSTING CREATURE

Without legal restrictions generally placed upon their sexual activity, lesbians don't often make it into the official record. This makes researching a difficult task as one needs to look for subtle clues. There are, however, a couple of stories I know of though they do need further research.

What, for example, is one to make of the friendship of Anne Drysdale and her younger companion, Caroline Elizabeth Newcombe? For twelve years from 1841, they farmed and lived together on land on the Barwon River in Victoria. Both strict Methodists, they seem to have lived an exemplary life marked by 'a zealous observance of all the ordinances of religion'. Yet, it was only after the death of her older companion and business partner that Newcombe, at the age of forty-nine, married a local Wesleyan minister. And, when she died in 1874, it was her wish to be buried beside her old friend and not her husband. What are we to make of this relationship?

And what of Des Tooley? She was a 1930s jazz night club singer known as the 'lady baritone' because of her deep voice. It is said that she and her pianist were inseparable companions, but little beyond this is known.

As with gay men, some lesbians in the inter-war period, sometimes because of illegal activities, were noticed by the police, and particularly by Sydney's first policewoman, Lillian Armfield. She worked tirelessly to stamp out 'sexual deviation'.

There was one area of employment which attracted her particular interest and this provides a clue to the researcher. She stated —

> In some of the city's biggest department stores several
> women have been blacklisted because of this activity
> [lesbianism]. They have sought jobs among a lot of girls for
> the sole purpose of selecting likely converts to their
> perversion.

Armfield's biographer, Vince Kelly, gives another important clue when he goes on to claim that many women educated into forms of sexual deviation 'come to Sydney from other States, and are usually in contact with each other in special groups.'

Just what 'special groups' there were in Sydney in the inter-war period is yet to be revealed.

Best of all, however, there is the story of Iris Webber, the person

Iris Webber, sexual deviationist

Armfield called 'a sexual deviationist [who] boasted of her activities as a lesbian.' She also labelled her 'Sydney's most violent woman criminal.'

Iris Webber seems to have moved with ease through the underworld of gangs, sly grog shops and prostitution which were so much part of East Sydney life before and after the Second World War. She wasn't in the class of the infamous underworld figures Kate Leigh and Tilly Devine. Iris Webber was regarded as more of a petty criminal.

However, the police were wary of her. She possessed enormous strength and had a hair-trigger temper. One example of this, if perhaps a little exaggerated, is told by Vince Kelly —

> When she was operating a sly grog shop in Darlinghurst she
> attacked a man who had come to buy some liquor because
> he queried her price. In a flash she picked up a meat
> chopper and rushed at him. Before he could protect

himself, she had slashed both his wrists so badly that the man ... lost the use of his arms from the elbows down almost completely.

She was also very intelligent. On one occasion Lillian Armfield had her up in court on a charge of 'sexual deviation' by which would seem to be meant the corruption of a minor. Iris successfully defended herself much to the annoyance of police. Later, she is said to have boasted, 'No girl under twenty-five is any use to me'.

As would be expected, Armfield believed her to be 'a horrible woman, a disgusting creature, completely without shame or conscience'.

I confess the more I read this sort of response the more interesting Iris Webber becomes. More does need to be researched on her life, but one further episode is worth recounting.

It would appear that she was affectionately and sexually involved with a woman who was a prostitute. This woman seems to have walked out on two men, well known gangsters, in order to live with Iris Webber. Kelly takes up the story, in his usual 'purple prose' style —

When each went wrathfully to get his woman back, Iris Webber was good and ready. They found her armed and ready to shoot it out on their own terms. Her violence appalled even these men who were case-hardened, and she sent them flying from her home with bullets whizzing about them.

Now there's a role model!

SOURCE: *Australian Dictionary of Biography* Vol. 1, 1788-1850. 'Anne Drysdale' (Melbourne, 1966)
Vince Kelly, *Rugged Angel: The Amazing Career of Policewoman Lillian Armfield* (Sydney, 1961) pp. 77-84

IS THAT A PISTOL IN YOUR POCKET?

The Australian armed forces have always had difficulty accepting the fact of homosexual people in the services. The concern dates back even as far as the First World War.

The *Official History of Australia in the War* has this to say of the contribution of homosexual men and women to the war effort. Significantly, it is listed under the heading of 'Moral Perversions' within the Medical volume —

The Genetically Abnormal Mind.
The experience of the A.I.F. [Australian Infantry Forces] in
these very important matters was slight, so far at least as
records reveal. There is no evidence pointing to any
significant homosexuality in the force, and this is on a par
with Australian experience in general. The records of the
A.I.F. therefore provide no contribution to the place of the
homosexual in a total war effort.

The wording is curious but the assumption behind it is not. Homosexuality, it is saying, may be part of a decadent European civilisation but does not exist in a young, vigorous nation such as is Australia with all its open spaces, fresh air and sunshine. It, therefore, does not exist in the Defence Forces either.

We know, of course, that this is just so patently false.

Other writers did note that homosexuals had played their part in the war in defence of the British Empire. In his autobiography, *Viewless Winds*, Dr Herbert Moran had a less condemnatory view, but one which still expresses some of the common attitudes of the time. He was a medical doctor in the armed services —

We had for a contemporary a big chunk of a man whom we
admired for his qualities of grit and rugged determination.
He was not a great exponent [of football], lacking the
speed and cleverness necessary for the first flight, but in a
tight corner he shone resolute and inspiring. When the war

came he responded promptly, displaying the same qualities in the ranks as with his team. What a great try-out is the football ground!

This man, somewhat clumsy but amazingly strong, never flinched in either sport or war. He was wounded but volunteered a second time from Australia. Then one day we heard, to our dismay, that he had been arrested for soliciting boys in the streets; this masculine hero who had faced barbed wire and machine guns in France was a homosexualist. It came out that his perversion dated back to his college days, but loyal friends for years had guarded his secret.

By contrast with the official history of the First World War, that of the Second World War does not even touch upon the subject of homosexuality. The files, however, reveal one curious episode which occurred in 1943.

The Commander, New Guinea Force, wrote to Army Headquarters seeking advice as to how to deal with 'Homosexual Males'. He was advised that 'those addicted' should be sent to a psychiatrist and, after examination, possibly discharged. The New Guinea Commander then expressed concern that this could be used as a means of transfer from the war front by 'weak minded' individuals. It transpired that, following a US Army 'crackdown' on 'Sodomites' in early 1943, the names of several Australians had been passed on to the Australian Army in New Guinea, hence the concern. At about the same time as the letter from New Guinea was received, the Commanding Officer in Victoria had written to request similar advice. Headquarters, perhaps imagining that they were now dealing with a greater problem than they had at first thought, replied in more vigorous terms than previously; those people against whom evidence existed should be charged, and possibly gaoled, before discharge.

It was decided to undertake an investigation as to how many convictions for homosexuality there had been up to that date in the war. Requests were sent to all Commanders seeking information. When, however, by October 1944 it was discovered that there had only been two convictions in Western Australia, two in Queensland, one in the Northern Territory, three in New South Wales, two in South Australia and three in New Guinea, it was decided that this was a minor problem and no further action needed to be taken.

This is not to say that the Army, particularly at the unit level, was still not paranoid about the presence of homosexuals in the ranks. Something of the flavour of this is conveyed in Lawson Glassop's novel, *The Rats in New Guinea*. One soldier, a former radio announcer, is assigned to a unit. The immediate reaction is that, because of his 'pink face' and 'fruity voice', he must be homosexual and he is taunted thus by the other men. The unit commander is appalled, 'Surely Hemilton was not a queen. That was one thing you feared — having a queen in your section.'

The underlying assumption here, of course, is a correct one. There were many homosexual men and lesbians, other than those whose sexuality was found out or who were convicted of an offence, who served, fought and died in the Second World War and in earlier and later conflicts.

The Services, however, and the Returned Services League in particular, continue in their opposition to homosexuals serving in the military — a closed mind seems to be *de rigueur* for the military hierarchy. It was something of a shock therefore, and a cause of celebration, when the Federal Labor Government lifted the ban on gay men and lesbians joining the military forces in late 1992.

For once, the forces of enlightenment seem to have won.

SOURCES: AA (Vic). Department of Defence (III) Army Headquarters. MP 742/1, Correspondence files, 1943-51. *item*: 84/1/74
Herbert Moran, *Viewless Winds* (London, 1939) pp. 53-54
Lawson Glassop, *The Rats in New Guinea* (Sydney, 1963) pp. 20-21

THE MURDER OF STOKER RILEY

Stoker John Joseph Riley was brutally murdered. Just after half past seven on the evening of 12 March 1942, screams 'of a man apparently in pain' were heard coming from the forecastle deck on HMAS *Australia*, then on escort duty in the Pacific.

The cries gradually weakened. Riley was found lying on deck moaning and in a pool of blood. With at least 14 stab wounds in his back, chest and arms, and with liver and lung damage, he was carried to the sick bay. He lapsed into a coma and within twenty-six hours was dead. The ship's log records that at 5.13 pm on 14 March, he was buried at sea somewhere off Noumea.

The crew members who rushed to Riley's assistance found that two others were already there — Leading Stoker Albert G. and Stoker Edward E. One of them was splashed with blood. Witnesses later said that several minutes before the screams were heard, G. and E. had been in the company of an unidentified 'third man', later believed to be Riley. Subsequently, these two seamen were charged with Riley's murder.

I first became intrigued by this murder some years ago when shown a manuscript of reminiscences by Clive Madigan. While Madigan's story was told with graphic detail, it unfortunately lacked some specific facts — such as the names of those involved. Then in mid-1988, in the course of my archival work, I found myself in contact with the Navy's legal branch. In passing, I enquired whether my contact had heard of such a case. He had. It was famous for its legal aspects. My interests, of course, lay elsewhere.

I keyed the names into the Australian Archives' computer and, to my delight, it revealed that there were three legal files on open access in the Melbourne Office. It was not until November 1989 that I was finally able to get to Melbourne to see them. By this time I had already viewed the ship's log in the Sydney Office, but it proved to be disappointingly short on detail. Just why, I was later to discover.

Of the three files, the largest and most important concerned the court-martial and subsequent events. It was with this that I began.

At the court-martial, held over four days from 15 April, witness after witness gave testimony that three men had been seen struggling at the scene of the crime, but no one could give a positive identification of all three, particularly of Riley.

G. and E. claimed that they had heard screams and had come to Riley's assistance, and that they had seen two other unidentified men running from the scene. In the end, the weight of circumstantial evidence pointed to them having murdered Riley. They were found guilty and sentenced —

> to be hanged by the neck till they be dead on board one of His Majesty's Australian ships and at such time as the Board for Naval Administration for Naval Forces shall direct.

This was the only sentence open to the court once the defendants had been found guilty.

Now the curious and interesting thing about the court-martial is that proceedings were confined to statements of fact alone. At no stage was the question of a motive for the crime ever raised in the court. Indeed, as the file makes clear, all questions of motive were 'rigorously excluded' from the trial, and this with the tacit approval of the defence counsel.

Yet, despite his condition and before he lapsed into a coma, Riley had spoken to the ship's surgeon. He had given information which later was passed on to Captain Armstrong, the ship's commander. Armstrong himself carried out the murder investigation under (in his own words) 'a certain amount of third degree conditions'.

So what, I wondered, had happened to the individual statements of the crew members gathered by Captain Armstrong? They apparently said much about the circumstances surrounding the murder, and no doubt held the clue as to the motive for it. Why were they no longer in the files? It would seem that they could have been removed sometime before the files were transferred to the archives. One possible reason for such an action is that the Navy itself had something to hide.

Once a sentence of death had been passed by a court-martial, it had to be ratified by the War Cabinet. The defence counsel immediately submitted to the Minister for the Navy 'a statement in mitigation of the death sentence passed'. In this statement, he made much of 'the abnormality of the present times' and added that this was 'likely to produce a warped state of mind in certain men.'

Other factors stressed were: the youth of the two seamen — Albert G. was 24, Edward E. 23; the 'monotonous and uncomfortable' conditions in which ratings were living and working below deck so that 'the softening influence of the opposite sex is accordingly absent'; and the brutalising effect of war 'in which life seems so cheap.' He concluded that —

> I am certain that the effect of two and a half years of these conditions in wartime is such to produce an abnormal, unnatural and perhaps perverse state of mind in some men so that they acquire a peculiar outlook which warps the reason and judgement.

From the direction of these arguments, I immediately suspected that there was a great deal more to this case than was at first evident. Understandably in time of war, none of this was made public at the time of the trial.

After their conviction, G. and E. had been transferred to Long Bay Gaol, Sydney, to await a decision on their sentence.

Meanwhile, the defence counsel made an appeal to the High Court, claiming that the court-martial had been wrongly constituted in law. The court had been convened under the British *Naval Discipline Act,* because in time of war the Australian armed forces were subject to United Kingdom legislation. The defence argued that the court should have been convened under the Australian *Defence Forces Act.* This was the main basis of the appeal (and the later legal interest). After a brief hearing, however, the appeal was dismissed.

This should have been the end of the case. But the fact that the appeal had taken place planted doubt in the public mind as to whether justice had been done. This was to provide the case with a bizarre twist.

The relatives of Albert G. and Edward E. began to agitate on behalf of the two prisoners. And they succeeded in gaining support from a wide cross-section of the community. Groups as diverse as the left wing Balmain branch of the Labor Party and the conservative Returned Services League, together with prominent individuals such as the Roman Catholic Archbishop of Sydney, Norman Gilroy, began to make representations on behalf of them.

The War Cabinet, soon after the High Court Appeal, had commuted the death sentence to one of life imprisonment. But this did not stop the agitation on behalf of the two sailors. So much so, in fact, that the government, by early 1944, was forced to set up an inquiry into the whole case. This step was, of course, vigorously opposed by the Navy.

Justice Maxwell of the New South Wales Supreme Court headed the Inquiry, which was held *in camera*. After due consideration had been given to the case, he recommended that the sentence of life imprisonment be reduced to twelve years. The naval establishment was displeased indeed. But, again, none of the evidence and deliberation in the Inquiry was made public.

Another of the files in the archives shows that by 1949 the supporters of G. and E. were again agitating on their behalf, seeking a further remission to their sentences on the grounds of good behaviour. Further, they were claiming that the two prisoners should be entitled to the general Peace Amnesty accorded to other prisoners.

The Naval Board was furious that the question should even be raised. But once more they were overruled. After consideration, it was agreed to grant remission to them.

The final file on the case concerns the details of their release. Albert G. was released from prison on 11 September 1950. Edward E. gained his freedom seven days later.

Now all this would seem to be a minor tale of young men cracking under the strain of war. But the very fact of the secrecy surrounding the court martial proceedings and the removal or lack of some evidence on file — particularly the crew's statements — confirmed for me that there was something unusual about this case. And there was.

One file still does contain a covering letter by Captain Armstrong, at almost the final folio, which summarises the information he gathered. From this it is clear that the murder was to do with homosexuality, but not in a way that you might at first think. Armstrong states that —

> the motive and basis of the crime would probably turn out
> to be found in certain alleged practices of unnatural vice
> which had been going on in the ship unknown to authority.

Of more interest, however, was Armstrong's next statement. It would seem that 'Riley had heard of the association between G. and E. and/or others [and] was trying to blackmail them.'

Riley's murder then, was a particularly nasty response by two presumably frightened men seeking to protect themselves, and possibly others.

Furthermore, at the *in camera* Inquiry into the sentence passed, in early 1944, four crew members were named as the 'others' in the case. All four had deserted from the ship within weeks of the court-martial. Though subsequently all were 'recovered from desertion', three were later discharged from the Navy — two, 'Services no longer required' and one, 'medically unfit.'

One wonders just how representative these 'others' were of that body of Australian seamen then on active service.

I am left with three responses to this case. The first is a certain amusement at the great irony in it. If the authorities had been less concerned to suppress any discussion of homosexuality for the sake of its public image, and had the motive for the murder been publicly known, then one can imagine how much popular support the case would have received. Almost none. Because it seems to have suppressed the evidence of possible scandal, the Navy actually assisted G. and E. to gain their freedom.

The case also annoys me. Much work is now being done in researching gay history, in reclaiming our past. One area of interest has been the lives of homosexuals in the armed services. Allan Berube's recently published book, *Coming Out Under Fire: Gays and Lesbians in World War II,* is an example. It is frustrating that evidence which could be vital to the study of homosexuality in our armed services — especially the depositions of the individuals interrogated by Captain Armstrong — has gone missing, presumably destroyed.

Finally, I am left with a great deal of curiosity as to what happened to Albert G. and Edward E., and the 'others', in their future lives. Fifty years on, does anyone know?

SOURCES: AA (Vic). Department of Defence. MP 742/1. *item*: 84/1/164, Homosexual Males [in Armed Forces during World War 11] Discharge, 1944 and MP 1587/1. *item:* 123v, Murder of Stoker JJ Riley, 1942-1944 and MP 1214/1. *item:* 445/201/230, [Murder of Stoker JJ Riley] 1942-1950 Allan Berube, *Coming Out Under Fire: Gays and Lesbians in World War II* (NY, 1990)

DRESSING UP!

The annual Sydney Gay & Lesbian Mardi Gras and Melbourne's MidSumma Festival have established themselves as part of our culture. Many would be surprised at just how long a tradition it is for members of the homosexual sub-cultures in Australia's cities to party and to dress up.

In both Melbourne and Sydney, there were large parties of homosexual men and lesbians, for example, on the Queen's Birthday holiday weekends in the Blue Mountains near Sydney, and at various locations in Melbourne. These parties had a long history, going back to well before the Second World War, and lasted until fairly recently in both cities. Other cities had similar celebrations beginning in a later period.

During the year, smaller local parties were also held regularly, sometimes at secret locations to avoid the attentions of the police. It was illegal for men to publicly dress in women's clothing until relatively recent times. Newspaper reporters seeking a sensational expose were also interested in such 'parties of the painted pansies', as the *Truth* newspaper referred to them.

I am constantly amazed by the ingenuity used in avoiding the attention of the police and the press. At one local party in the 1950s, for example, a band of blind musicians was hired for the night. There were no reports of illegal activity coming from that event!

Unfortunately, they were not always so successful. From court reports, however, we do gain some insight into the dress sense of homosexual men of fifty years ago.

In 1942, for example, police and MPs raided a party at a Scout Hall in the Sydney suburb of Annandale. Five men were arrested and appeared in court next day. Four of them were still in drag 'with their faces powered and their hair permed, though it was a shame', as the Sydney *Sunday Telegraph* reported, that 'nasty beards marred the otherwise glamorous appearance'.

The youngest of those arrested, an eighteen-year-old army deserter, was the most stylish dresser, 'Black velvet frock, beaded and

Virgil's drawing of the five young men who dressed as women at the dance

low cut, with fox furs. Earrings and a heavy matching silver necklet, gold anklets over sheer silk stockings, and high heel shoes.'

He was almost matched by the eldest of the group, a twenty-five-year old in a 'Bottle-green frock with vermilion yoke and sleeves, silk stockings, and high heeled shoes.'

Where they got the silk stockings during a time of war rationing we will probably never know. A friendly American soldier perhaps?

Each year in Sydney there was also the Artists' Ball (sometimes referred to the as the 'Drag & Drain' Ball). While these were not exclusively homosexual events, there are some wonderful gay stories connected with them.

One occasion during the war is recounted in Jon Rose's autobiographal novel, *At The Cross*. He goes to a house to meet with several friends before the Ball. Inside —

> Cliff and Dennis were dressed as Greek soldiers. Also in the house were ten other people, including two Carmen Mirandas, one of whom was frantically trying to turn herself into Dolores del Rio.

Finally, they got to the Ball —

> Inside the hall, the heat, the noise, the crush was fantastic. It was only midnight, but the ball was well away ... half the theatre and radio world seemed to be there ... Milly and I counted at least eight Carmen Mirandas, most of whom glared at one another ...

The police, as ever, intervened and raided the Ball. A drag queen,

Melba, had been singing when the police rushed in —
Melba, who'd nearly strangled on a high note, stood dead
centre of the stage, glaring. The leading cop walked down
the middle of the hall saying as he either walked over
people, or knocked them flying, "Come on down, you
poofter." Melba put her hand on her hip and said, "Just
supposing you come up and get me, you big bull." The
copper was furious and started yelling, "I told you to yet
down off there, you great bastard, I'll bash you black and
blue when you do." Melba waved her lorgnette saying, "Oh
you great big impetuous dream boy, why don't you come up
to Momma?" The cop glared and bellowed, "You're no
Momma, you'll never even be poppa." Melba flashed back,
"Really darling, l know you're upset, but that's no way to
speak to a dame." The copper, still trying to get over bodies,
almost shrieked, "Dame! dame? You're no dame you, you
big pervert." Melba yelled back "And you're no gent, and I'll
bet you're bloody lousy in bed as well."
And that second, a tremendous gale of screams rent the air,
as twenty-five show girls, getting dressed backstage, started
to get an inkling of what was happening in front. Before the
screams had died down, everything in the hall went mad:
cops started grabbing people, pulling off wigs, having a
look, then slamming a wig back on, and hauling the wig's
occupant towards the main doors. Then everyone yelled at
everyone else, and the leading cop kept trying to climb up
onto the stage, which was difficult for him, because he first
had to climb over the stunned orchestra who sat not
knowing whether to play, drop dead on the spot, or bash
him and his helpers with their instruments. Some eight feet
up, the stage also seethed with activity. Melba and her little
friend let the cops have the lot, everything they could lay
their hands on. The head cop and Melba fought it out, he
trying to climb up, she bashing him down with her
lorgnette. The little pianist threw music, her shoes, her wig,
and something that, frightened out of my wits as I was,
surprised me when I saw it fly overhead. Coming from
nowhere, it was a water melon. It hit a Betty Grable,
knocking her out on the spot. Just then Melba, with a
triumphant yell, crowned the cop with a pot of flowers.

In the post-war period the Artists' Balls continued to build on these traditions, though not all were as exciting as this one. And while there continued to be police surveillance, police harassment of the functions gradually ceased.

But there are still some remarkable stories. That, for example, of the man who dressed as a conductress, got on a tram at Railway Square, took fares all the way up George Street and then alighted at the Trocadero (now the site of the Hoyts Theatre) where the ball was being held.

Or the Drag Queen whose costume was so huge he had to hire a large truck with a back lift to transport him to the Ball!

Mardi Gras and MidSumma just continue a long tradition of our joyous rites of celebration. Of course we don't see too many Betty Grables or Carmen Mirandas on the dance floor these days. And not too many silk stockings are on show either.

SOURCES: Sydney *Sunday Telegraph,* 9 August 1942
Jon Rose, *At The Cross* (London, 1961)
Interview with Bill Robson, 1990

THE YELLOW SOX GANG

At the end of the Second World War, most major population centres in Australia had an established and thriving, though often small, homosexual sub-culture based around long-time friendship networks. Consisting of both homosexual men and lesbians, this close knit 'camp scene' had its own rites and rituals, such as 'camp marriages', the beats and sometimes, in larger centres, discrete bars. But, in the days of the 'six o'clock closing' of hotels most of the social activities centred on parties either at home or at larger venues on weekends, particularly Queen's Birthday holiday weekends.

In 1949 something of this hidden society was revealed to the world at large by journalist, later novelist, George Johnston in an article in *The Sun*, a Sydney newspaper —

> To a considerable extent, most of Sydney's homosexuals form an almost self-contained social section of the city, and to this community (in which most members are known to each other) there is a regular stream of new recruits ... Groups of individuals regularly correspond with, and are visited by, foreign seamen who themselves are homosexual ...
> Large so-called 'pansy parties' are held fairly regularly — sometimes with as many as 100 to 150 guests — but usually are much more intimate. At the much larger gatherings, it is sometimes the curious practice to invite a few women. They are invariably prostitutes and are never touched by the male guests. As one regular explained it:
> 'We have them along to provide a touch of exotic colour.'

Garry Wotherspoon, in his book, *City of the Plain,* has documented the post-war camp society of Sydney. But the coal mining and steel city of Newcastle, only a couple of hours to the north, also had its own sub-culture. While small, there seems to have only been one beat, its parties were nonetheless famous.

The 1950s, however, was also the period of the Cold War with its accompanying concerns with anything different from what was perceived as the norm. While the main fear was of communism, homosexual men and women were sometimes caught up in the paranoia.

On 20 October 1951, the *Sydney Morning Herald* reported comments by New South Wales Police Superintendent Colin Delaney that police were alarmed that male homosexuality was 'on the increase'. The police reacted by increasing entrapment procedures, which led to an increase in the number of arrests. This in turn led Delaney seven years later, and by then New South Wales Police Commissioner, to make the amazing statement that homosexuality was 'Australia's greatest menace and fastest growing crime'. To otherwise law-abiding homosexual men of the time it was the vicious police entrapment procedures which were the real menace.

Against this background the 'spectre' of homosexuality was frequently blown out of all proportion. A perfect example is the story of the Newcastle yellow sox gang.

In June 1952, it was reported that detectives from Sydney's Criminal Investigation Bureau and the military police had assisted in the arrest of 'eight homosexual men ranging in age form 17 to 35' on charges of offensive behaviour and buggery. Other arrests followed.

Most of the men were part of the homosexual sub-culture in Newcastle at the time. Three, however, were soldiers from the Holsworthy army camp outside Sydney. Later in court one army arrestee gave evidence of having been invited to a party after an encounter with a Newcastle man on a Sydney Harbour ferry. This military connection may well explain how the authorities cottoned onto the scene.

Some weeks later, the charges were heard in the Supreme Court sitting in Newcastle. The lawyers in the court fuelled excitement about the case with the sensationalist claim that 'A society of perverts, membership of which was quite large, existed in Newcastle.'

Judge Brereton agreed. He said —

> The offences should serve as an awakening that
> homosexuality was rife in the city and district to a degree
> which he had never dreamed of, and he was sure other
> people had never heard of.

These were extraordinary statements at the start of what, I think, became an extraordinary court case.

All defendants pleaded 'Guilty'. Indeed it was admitted in Court that they had not been 'caught' as such. Once the existence of the group had become known to police, its members had all 'confessed' during interview and 'if there had been no confessions there would have been no charges'. [!]

This, presumably, applied also to the seventeen year old defendant, whom one detective described as being a 'confirmed pervert'. As a minor, his case would have been heard in the Children's Court, thus the details are not available.

Information given in court does give clues as to the type of camp scene it was. The background of most defendants was mainly working, or lower middle, class. One was an apprentice typewriter mechanic, another a Post Office technician, a third was a storeman-packer, two others were a salesmen and another a mercer, who owned a men's clothing store. Of the soldiers, one had a background as a printer, another was an army cook.

The evidence describing their social gatherings is not unlike that described earlier by George Johnston. In speaking about one of the defendants, the storeman-packer who lived in the inner Sydney suburb of Redfern, Detective Landkin said —

> He was invited to perform a theatrical act at a hall in
> Newcastle where a function was run by sex perverts. As a
> result of his association with these people ... He made
> subsequent visits to Newcastle and met the men referred to
> in the charges ...
> Membership of the group of perverts was quiet large. They
> met in halls in Newcastle and in homes ... Quite a number
> of them have left the district.

In the light of what happened to those arrested, one could hardly blame them!

Throughout the case there was some support given to the men by members of the wider Newcastle community. For example, a 'bricklaying contractor' gave evidence as to the good character of one defendant. He said that he had know him all his life and that he 'had eliminated the offence since his arrest'. Another witness, a master printer, attested to 'the excellent character' of another of the defendants.

The police, presumably having already decided who were the evil instigators and who were the victims, also gave evidence as to the good character of some defendants. Detective Landkin said of one of the soldiers that if he 'had kept away from Newcastle, he would have been alright'. The horrified judge then responded —

Do you suggest that this type of offence is peculiar to Newcastle?

No, replied the Detective, but there seems to have been a group of them here.

I hope, his Honour replied, by the number of offences that have been brought before the Court that there are not many left.

It is the statements of the doctors, of course, which give a clue as to how homosexuality was then viewed and characterised by the medical profession. One doctor, in supporting a defendant said he had 'a 60-40 percentage of masculinity and femininity in his make-up'.

Of another it was said that —

To overcome his tendencies, it would be necessary to re-educate him. He would have to be taken from the home environment and introduced to manly sports such as could be obtained at clubs like the Police Boy's Club.

But contemporary opinion, based upon medical opinion, seems to have been best expressed by one defence lawyer, 'It seems from what medical men say that these tendencies are born in people. They are, in other words, 'off the Beam'.

Actually, this is a fairly enlightened view for the times. Of course, a plea was being made that they should not be gaoled.

By the end of the case, His Honour was well and truly astounded by the all the evidence and expressed the opinion that 'this is beginning to read like the stories we read of Germany after the first war'.

Nonetheless, he agreed with defence counsel, at least in the case of the majority of the defendants. Most were given a two year suspended sentence and a twenty pound bond. Four, however, were sent to gaol. The 33-year-old sales assistant and the thirty-year-old mercer, presumably being older, were seen as having led the others astray. Of the two soldiers imprisoned, one already had spent time in an army prison for other offences.

But why yellow sox? Well it would seem that the mercer who was gaoled sold yellow sox to his camp clientele. As Jim Wafer of the Newcastle Gay & Lesbian Social History Project, has written, 'The socks became a means of mutual recognition in any context, not just at the beat.'

It was as a result of the court case and this local dress code that the spectre of 'the yellow sox gang' entered Newcastle mythology. To the extent it did is illustrated by a quote from a 1968 book on the history of the city —

> There was a gang of homosexuals who rocked the town in the middle fifties when their number and names were revealed in a spectacular court case — the famous Yellow Sox Boys. Their pass sign was a pair of yellow socks or a yellow tie, and to this day yellow socks are virtually taboo in Newcastle.

At the launch of the Centre for Gay and Lesbian Research at the University of Sydney by Bill Hayden, Governor-General of Australia, on 25 June 1993, it was pleasing to see that a contingent had come from Newcastle upholding their regional traditions. They were all wearing matching yellow sox and ties!

SOURCES: George Johnston, 'Predatory Men Worst Blot in City's Growing Vice' Sydney *The Sun,* 15 June 1949 p. 3
Newcastle Morning Herald, 20 June and 8 July 1952
A Farrelly & R Morrison, *Newcastle* (Sydney 1968) p. 61
Jim Wafer to Robert French, 9 June 1993

PRETTY POLICEMEN

Police entrapment of homosexual men, as we have seen, has a history going back to the 1920s. With homosexual sub-cultures well established by then in most major cities, the police had discovered 'the homosexual' as 'menace'. The homosexual community had their own terms for the police such as 'lily law'. Later, they referred to them as 'pretty policemen' because of their entrapment techniques. These included sending young policemen, out of uniform, to beats in an attempt to solicit an advance, and, in more recent times, even to engage in sexual activity. The hapless victim of course, was then arrested but seldom was the police activity ever questioned.

People so arrested (even people who were committing no 'offence' at all) often had their lives ruined by the experience unless (sometimes with the help of a solicitor) they could get away with pleading guilty, hoping for a fine and no publicity.

There are, however, three interesting cases in Sydney where people who have been arrested for offensive behaviour in public toilets have disputed the police case in court, and won.

In 1943, Clarence McNulty, then editor of the *Daily Telegraph*, was arrested for 'wilfully and obscenely exposing his person' in the toilet in Lang Park in the city. McNulty, a married man with a young family, strenuously denied the charge and engaged one of Sydney's top barristers, Mr Dovey QC, to appear for him.

The case came to court in February. Immediately the defence barrister went on the attack. He questioned the method the two arresting police used in making the arrest. It would seem that only one of the two police officers had entered the toilet, had approached McNulty and, on the basis of his version of events, made the arrest. Dovey put it to the police that the junior officer had 'acted as a decoy by entering the public lavatory for the purpose of aiding and abetting alleged offenders'.

Further, he seemed to imply that the police had an arrangement with a solicitor, who 'has appeared for more of these cases than any other single solicitor'.

It would seem that the police were zealous in entrapping people. They charged them, then appeared sympathetic to their plight and recommended a solicitor who would represent them in court. They

"Truth," 20/2/43 Page 8

Policeman Denies Acting As Decoy

SEARCHING EXAMINATION IN THE McNULTY CASE

A HEATED denial that he acted as a decoy, by entering public lavatories for the purpose of aiding and abetting alleged offenders so that he could arrest them was given by Constable Neville William Grigg, during the hearing of the case against Clarence Sydney McNulty, (43), Editor-in-Chief of the "Daily Telegraph," who pleaded not guilty in Central Police Court (Sydney) recently to a charge of wilful and obscene exposure. Grigg said that, with Constable Carney, he had made 900 arrests in a year, out of which number about 200 were for sexual offences. He had never apprehended an innocent person or advised the people he caught to plead guilty so as to avoid publicity.

GRIGG was questioned at some length regarding his association with Harold Munro, a solicitor. He admitted having met Munro on two occasions socially, but emphatically denied that he had ever received money for recommending solicitors. He had never instructed Munro to represent him in any matter, nor had he ever paid the solicitor any money, he said.

CHARGED AS "McNALLY"

McNulty was originally charged [name, age, occupation, religion and the name of any] under the name of Charles McNally, his address was taken [person other than] and was described in that charge as [the name of the] a clerk. His correct name and occupation were described by his counsel, Mr. Dovey, K.C., when the case was adjourned previously.

The charge alleged that Charles McNally, alias Clarence Sydney McNulty, 43, wilfully and obscenely exposed himself in a lavatory at Lang Park, City on January 9.

Mr A. W. Barry, Assistant Crown Solicitor, appeared on behalf of Constable Carney and Constable Grigg, concerned in the arrest of McNulty.

Mr. Dovey was assisted by Mr. B. A. Webb.

Grigg, in giving evidence, said he was 22 years old, and had been four years in the force. At 10.30 p.m. on January 9 he and Carney were in plainclothes in Grosvenor Street watching the public lavatory in Lang Park, and the lavatory in the public court.

Under cross-examination by Mr. Dovey, Grigg said that he had been in plainclothes for the past 12 months. Before that he had done uniform duty and had worked with the S.P. squad.

Grigg said that apart from working interests of justice might be served by this public hearing and the announcement of names? It is unfortunate for the individuals, but beyond that there is a public principle.

Mr. Dovey (to Grigg): Will you admit that with, perhaps, eight or

King, the Station Sergeant, took him to the bail would be £20.

"I know it to stop if I know of my own experience where evidence is most saved a man's neck. How do we know but that the [sent some person we have arrested and we have pointed that person out] So apparently the solicitor didn't know his client?—That is how it would appear to me.

Have you ever received money for recommending solicitors?—No.

Frequently when men are arrested and then remanded they deposit a cash bail?—Yes.

CLARENCE SYDNEY McNULTY, 43-year-old editor-in-chief of Consolidated Press Ltd., publishers of the Daily and Sunday "Telegraph" and "Woman's Weekly," who faces a charge of wilful and obscene exposure.

"It seems most surprising that a man is arrested and charged in some place before the court and then someone takes it upon himself to absolve the man of the charge," he said. "It was a great pity that such a position arose."

When Mr. Dovey suggested that the matter was one that did not affect the case, Mr. McCulloch retorted that he had every right to comment upon any irregular practice.

Mr. Dovey questioned Grigg intensively regarding his association with Harold Munro, solicitor.

Grigg said he had met Munro socially — once at the theatre and once at Carney's home. He denied that he was in the habit of drinking with Munro. He knew Munro's managing clerk, Mr. Kelly. He had met him at Munro's office.

Mr. Dovey: What were you doing there?

Grigg: I went with Carney about seven months ago when Carney had a will made out. I subsequently returned when Carney signed the will. Weren't you and Carney with Munro in the Balfour Hotel one evening you were suspended, January 18?—I was in the Balfour. I don't think I had a drink. We went there looking for Munro.

Grigg said he did not instruct Munro to appear for him in any matter, and did not pay him any money. These were the only occasions on which he had met Munro.

Mr. Dovey: Didn't you see him last night?

Grigg: Yes, I overlooked that. Were you at Carney's place at night when Munro visited there?—I think I was there when Munro visited on the 18th.

Mr. McCulloch: Thinking to be good. You as a constable ought to know that. Thinking takes me nowhere. I may as well tell the detective clerk not to put it down.

were urged to plead guilty, pay the fine and hope for no publicity. The whole matter would be hushed up and no one questioned police methods. The Police gained a successful arrest and the solicitor another case. One presumes also, though I have no evidence, that money changed hands between solicitor and police. Quite a nice little rort!

In the McNulty case the police came unstuck because their version of events was challenged and, more importantly, because of their methods. According to police procedure both officers should have entered the toilet. Because only one did so, the case came down to a dispute between two individuals.

The magistrate gave McNulty the benefit of the doubt and discharged him. At the same time, the court insisted on —

> expressing the opinion that there had been definite perjury on one side or the other, but [was] unable to determine whether the defence or prosecution had been lying.

The magistrate was furious with the police officers because both failed to enter the toilet, one presumes not because it would have aided the defendant's case but because their corroborated evidence would have secured a conviction. It was then very rare for any magistrate, often former police prosecutors themselves, ever to question police evidence in court.

Ten years later, a similar case gained wide media coverage in Sydney, again because an individual concerned was prepared to stand up to the police and their tactics.

Douglas Annand was a well know graphic artist. He produced the famous 1938 Sequi-Centenary poster of the lifesaver with a banner standing under the Sydney Harbour Bridge.

In 1952, he was arrested in a toilet in Chatswood Park and charged with 'soliciting a male for immoral purposes'. He not only pleaded not guilty in court, but took out a five thousand pound writ against the police for damages.

Despite his denial of the charge, he was found guilty. Annand appealed.

The Appeal, before Judge Neild, caused a sensation. Not only did the judge quash the conviction but he criticised the Magistrate. However, it was the police who came in for his most severe criticism. The judge accused the arresting police officer of fabricating his story with two other officers and said his statement was 'a wretched lie … I disbelieve the whole of his evidence'.

The arresting policeman was immediately suspended from duty.

The third case concerned the famous pianist Claudio Arrau. He was accused, in 1957, of soliciting a policemen by 'winking' at him. Again the 'offence' took place in the Lang Park toilet. Arrau was found guilty but also appealed. The appeal judge, while stating that the 'offence' could have been committed nonetheless dismissed the case as being utterly trivial.

These were very rare outcomes. Few people, especially homosexual men, were prepared to take cases so far. Most just paid their fine and, if they were lucky, could avoid exposure and get on with their lives.

But was it justice?

SOURCES: Melbourne *Truth* 20, 27 February and 13 March 1943
Sydney Morning Herald 20 December 1952 and 8 April, 27 July 1953
Sydney Morning Herald 28 July 1957 and 28 February 1958
Garry Wotherspoon, *City of the Plain* (Sydney, 1990) pp. 122-3

READ ALL ABOUT IT!

It was only in 1958 that the term 'homosexuality' made its first appearance (between 'home' and 'honey'!) as a subject heading in the *Sydney Morning Herald's* published *Quarterly Index*. This signals the beginnings of a general coverage of matters homosexual by the 'quality press'.

Of course, the 'yellow press', particularly the *Truth* newspaper, had been publishing articles on the subject since the 1920s. But these were usually sensationalist reports centred on court cases. The reporting in the quality press, however, far from being the dawn of a new enlightenment, simply reiterated all the old prejudices of a British colonial society, spiced with a dash of American witch-hunt mentality.

Initially the major stories of the decade were from Britain. Many had to do with the now-infamous spy scandals of the period. This was the era of Cold War paranoia, of Burgess and MacLean, and of Senator Joseph McCarthy. Western governments became obsessed about people differing from the norm, especially if they were suspected of being 'queers' or 'pooftas' to use the American, British and Australian slang words for homosexuals. The existence of homosexuals in the government, the armed forces and the church was believed to create 'a special problem'. Quoting a British Medical Association report of the early 1950s, one newspaper stated, 'Homosexuals had a tendency to place their loyalty to one another above their loyalty to institutions, or the government they served'.

The following are some examples of the many 'gay' scandals which surfaced in newspapers in the 1950s. While some of the incidents reported and the attitudes they reflect seem almost ludicrous by today's standards, they often had serious, and sometimes tragic, consequences on the lives of those they affected.

In 1953 Lord Montagu, 'the darling of Mayfair Society' and sometime escort to Princess Margaret, was charged with grave offences against Boy Scouts. He and two others were subsequently tried and sent to prison. At the same time Sir John Gielgud was arrested on 'a charge of having persistently importuned men at Chelsea', and Sir John Field MP was forced to resign from the House of Commons for a similar reason. Gielgud at least got off with a ten pound fine for being drunk and disorderly, though the magistrate was 'sceptical'.

These arrests, however, were not isolated incidents and it was Australian journalist Donald Horne who revealed why in an article in the Sydney *Sunday Telegraph*. The new Commissioner of Scotland Yard, Sir John Nott-Bower, had implemented, with government support, a plan to 'smash homosexuality in London'.

More importantly, Horne revealed, 'The plan originated under strong United States advice to Britain to weed out homosexuals — regarded as being hopeless security risks — from important government jobs'.

Already *Truth*, in April 1950, had reported a crackdown on lesbians and homosexual men in federal employment in Washington. Four thousand were investigated 'forcing the resignation of 91 homosexuals because the U.S. government deemed them security risks'. It was believed that a link existed between 'men and women perverts and Soviet espionage'.

Despite its links with overseas security organisations, particularly in the United Kingdom, the Australian Security Intelligence Organisation (ASIO) seems to have been more concerned with communists and trades unionists than with homosexuals. I have not been able to locate any file from the 1950s which specifically dealt with the topic. I suspect it was only in the 1960s, possibly following the much publicised prosecution in 1962 of William John Vassel (a cypher clerk in the United Kingdom Naval Attache's office in the Moscow Embassy) that ASIO and the Australian Government became generally concerned with the possibility of homosexuals as security risks. It was about this time, as Richard Hall reports, that Prime Minister Robert Menzies directed 'no homosexual is to have access to classified documents'.

Mind you, this is still a softer approach than dismissing them from government service altogether.

Of course, as we have seen, there were always people in authority in the 1950s, like New South Wales Police Commissioner Delaney, who took on the 'problem' of homosexuality as a personal crusade.

The police and judiciary in Melbourne expressed similar views. In 1954, Victorian Police Commissioner Duncan complained that the Police Offences Act was not adequate enough to allow people to be charged. As the Melbourne *Truth* reported it —

> Unless the 'twilight men' are actually caught committing an indecent act police cannot sustain charges. Even the creatures who masquerade in women's clothing are extremely difficult to convict because of the law's loopholes.

The following year, *Truth* carried another story headed 'Upsurge of Male Vice Alarms Police, Judges' in which it stated that, 'Police report that homosexuality has reached frightening limits, and because of the staggering increase in the last few years is now a major problem.'

Actually this type of reporting was typical of the times. In the 'yellow press', the 'spectre' of homosexuality was frequently blown

He Dressed Himself As A Glamor Girl
To Keep His Own Date
With Death

MOST macabre death in South Australia for many years has lurking behind it a compensating macabre story, revealed recently when police broke down the door of room No. 16, on the second floor of a Port Pirie hotel. Starkly meeting their gaze was the 12-hour lifeless body of 56-year-old piano tuner Herbert James Hutchins, hanging from the window, the blind cord of which was twisted tightly round his throat. Fantastically enough, police for a moment were baffled. They had broken in to find Hutchins; instead, at first glance, they found a woman; it was Hutchins decked out as a glamor girl, with all her fripperies if not fineries. Investigation eventually satisfied the wonder of the discoverers; Hutchins, in grotesque draperies of death, was revealed as a pathological subject all too familiar to students of abnormal psychology.

PIANO TUNER'S
MACABRE DEATH

PORT PIRIE police are definite now that, although Hut- clothing, he had only a few pounds in his possession, sufficient, said the police, to give this strange character

Just Looked At Him

IT was probably the way in which Lois Collier looked at him that made a Universal talent scout get out a pen and a dotted line and say, "Sign here!" By study in voice and drama- Her, Lois was already a polished radio performer.

out of all proportion throughout the 1950s and into the 1960s. The general tenor of newspaper reporting can easily be seen from some of the headlines: *Male Vice is a Threat to Civilisation, The Shame of Sydney, Upsurge in Male Vice Alarms Police, The Spreading Cult of the Homosexual, Boy's Frocks Shocked Cops, Big Names in Vice Net*, and *Immorality Rife in Big Charity*. In almost all these stories homosexuals were portrayed as sick, perverted criminals.

In England, the scandals led to the establishment of the

Wolfenden Committee and eventually, in 1967, to limited homosexual law reform.

In Australia, the best example of a government response to the 'problem' of homosexuality is that of the State Government in New South Wales. In June 1954, the *Truth* newspaper reported favourably that the New South Wales *Crimes Act* was to be amended providing 'for heavier penalties for male perverts'. And indeed in 1955 the New South Wales Justice Minister announced —

> the introduction of a homosexual bill to deal sociologically
> with the problem of homosexuality and to establish a
> committee to study its causes and cures. [!]

The Trethowan Committee, as it was called, was greeted by the *Sydney Morning Herald* with a favourable editorial —

> Sex offenders present a terrible and growing evil in the
> community. They are on the increase, and the Police
> Commissioner last year complained of the lack of power to
> deal with homosexuals. The first stage of reform is
> necessarily efficient policing to detect offenders.

At the same time it admitted —

> Ordinary imprisonment serves absolutely no purpose except
> that of preventing a repetition of the offence for just as long
> as the culprit is shut up.

It urged a 'sympathetic attempt to rehabilitate the offender'. For this 'special institutions are needed and a panel of doctors rather than a court of law should be the authority to decide when the offender can safely be released'. The *Sydney Morning Herald* was opting for a medical approach to 'the problem', a view which would gain popularity into the 1960s.

As appalling as we now find this, it was reasonably enlightened for its time, especially compared to the response of government. The Trethowan Committee investigating 'causes and cures' never reported. It is believed that the Committee could not agree with the support by some members for law reform proposals similar to that recommended by the United Kingdom's Wolfenden Committee. Despite a 1963 newspaper story that the Committee was about to issue a report, none was ever forthcoming.

One area where the quality newspapers did serve a useful purpose was through their letters columns. For example, following Commissioner Delaney's comments in 1958 about homosexuals being 'Australia's Greatest Menace', the *Sydney Morning Herald* carried letters not only for but also against his opinion. One correspondent rightly pointed out, 'The great increase in convictions is due not to any natural increase in homosexuality but to the increased zeal of the police in obtaining offences.' The same writer went on to condemn the use of police entrapment procedures.

The letters columns therefore presented a forum of opinion which was more varied than that expressed by the media in news stories. Though it is arguable just how influential this might have been, at least alternative opinions to perceived truths were being aired. And there is another important point to note.

Ironically, the more the newspapers reported on homosexuality the less isolated gay people generally became. They were made aware that they were not the only ones in the world. Furthermore,

THEY'RE HARD TO PICK

Perverts roam at night

By a Sun Reporter

Three times in the past week—in widely separated parts of Sydney — I have been accosted by perverts, and have come to a discouraging realisation.

If any one of those three perverts were put in a line-up, I would defy anybody to pick him as such.

There were no characteristics—that I could discern, anyway—to distinguish them from thousands of those "average citizens" I see daily.

So there we have a basic problem.

The three occasions were in a hotel lounge, on a 16-minute ferry trip, and while waiting for a woman to finish a telephone conversation. And they all occurred at night.

Asked for match

There was nothing about the approach to make me wary.

Two of them asked for a match, and I had made it easier for the other one by asking HIM for a match.

There is no purpose in pointing to a moral here. Nothing is more ordinary than being "bitten" for a light.

The popular conception of a pervert is recognisable in the antics of stage comedians — good for a laugh.

He is characterised by mincing gait, lisping voice, perfume and nail varnish.

And HE is the same anywhere—on the stage.

Sydney bookshops are featuring the latest memoirs of Scotland Yard's ex-Vice Squad Chief, Robert Fabian, who says with conviction born of years in London's underworld, "I can tell you a fair amount about perverts. . ."

So CAN I.

With a conviction born of a few months in Sydney.

Cottage destroyed

A five-roomed unoccupied weatherboard cottage in Moore Lane, Balmain, was destroyed by fire last night.

Elcon Food Mixers with easiest of terms. Ring M4579.★

SHAPELY actress Janet Leigh models a clinging gown of white lace over nude crepe. High neck and long, tight sleeves accentuate the lacy outline.

stories headlined *Perverts in the Park* (Melbourne) and *Park Haunt of Perverts* (Sydney) told isolated gay men where they could go to meet others, no matter how dangerous it might be to seek them out.

As bad, then, as newspaper reports on homosexuality in the 1950s may have been, they did begin the discussion which, decades later, established the climate of opinion in which gay liberation movements would surface and law reform could be achieved.

SOURCES: Sydney *Sunday Telegraph*, 25 October 1953

AA (ACT). ASIO. CRS A6122/26. *item*: 1194, Policy or Directives about the employment of homosexuals, 1949-1958

Richard Hall, *The Secret State* (Sydney, 1978) p. 60

Robert French, *Gays Between the Broadsheets: Australian Media References on Homosexuality, 1948-1980* (Sydney, 1986)

Robert French, 'Gay Issues in the Australian Press: 1953 to the Present' *Gay Information No. 6*, 1981 pp. 14-16

GENTLEMEN, I AM A HOMOSEXUAL

It began as a simple customs-related raid in Adelaide but ended with three people in Sydney being gaoled for homosexual offences and a world-wide search for members of a 'pen-friends club'.

In September 1959, officers of the Commonwealth Investigation Service (CIS) — parts of which were later subsumed into the Australian Security Intelligence Organisation and into the Federal Police — called at a house in an Adelaide suburb. The occupant was a 26-year-old man, who lived with his parents, and whose identity has been expunged from the public copy of the archival record to protect his privacy. For the purposes of this chapter I shall call him 'Brian'.

The officers had with them a tape-recording that had been sent to Brian from the Channel Islands in the United Kingdom. The tape had been seized as a prohibited import by customs officers working within the Post Office.

Brian told them that he frequently corresponded with his United Kingdom contact and that they had been put in touch through the Popular Pen Friends Club run by a J. S. Stanton in London. He also admitted that he corresponded with other club members around the world.

They engaged in conversation for awhile and after some straight forward questioning, Brian admitted that he had eight other tapes in his possession. Only at this point did the officers produce a search warrant and inform him that they intended to search his room.

As he led them there, he made a statement of what would have been obvious to them from the contents of the tape: 'Gentlemen, I might as well tell you now, I am a homosexual'.

The officers later reported —

> He took us to his room, which was very untidy and
> cluttered up with gramophone records, books, magazines,
> radiogram etc. We proceeded to search, and at intervals

discovered three more tapes which he said he had overlooked. Several albums of photographs were found and also a number of manila folders containing files of correspondence from numerous people in the United States, Canada, United Kingdom, Singapore and Australia. We confiscated the correspondence and photographs, together with copies of magazines. We also discovered photographs of nude males who he knows by name.

They also found a Boy Scout kit on top of the wardrobe and several current Boy Scout Magazines. When questioned, he admitted to once belonging to the movement but said he was no longer active in it.

The officers took the material away. On the next afternoon, however, they returned at Brian's request. He had found a further tape which he handed over. 'A search was also made of another room, in which was photography equipment and a tape recorder. Nothing of an objectional [sic] nature was found in that room.'

In commenting on the confiscated records, the officers pointed particularly to a number of special items (later to become court exhibits) — 'a folder initialled 'H' dated 24/11/58, in which reference is made to draped nude photographs which can be wiped with a damp cloth, thus removing the drape effect and exposing the complete nude figure', also a letter from New York enclosing 'press cuttings re police smashing an international pornography ring.'

Brian was cooperative throughout the investigation exhibiting (perhaps cleverly feigning?) naivety and denying any knowledge of wrong-doing, as the following exchange illustrates —

Were you not aware that it is an offence to send or receive indecent photographs or other goods through the post?
No.
You denied yesterday that you had sent photographs through the post. There is reference in some of the letters to you in reply to yours about a photograph of a Turkish boy which you had sent.
Oh. I only loaned the photos. You will find the Turkish boy's photo in an album. They were sent back to me.
Did you actually send indecent photographs through the post?
Yes.
When further questioned he stated that —

he obtained photos from the different publishers by selecting them from lists previously supplied to him. The photos were then sent out singly with letters and later placed in his album and indexed. It has been ascertained that the Good Companion, from whom introductory addresses were received, advertised in Man's World and their address is 33 Middle Street, Brighton, United Kingdom.

The officers then recommended that —

a thorough check of the seized material is advisable in order to ascertain various sources of supply of photographs etc. and information regarding other known homosexuals in other States who are probably receiving material of a similar nature.

Brian was prosecuted in the Adelaide Police Court on two charges of being in possession of prohibited imports, namely one tape recording and 60 photographs. He was convicted and fined fifty pounds with counsel fees of five pounds ten shillings court costs, a hefty amount for the time. Still he can probably be considered lucky given the further repercussions of the raid.

These were immense. It can be presumed, though the file in the Australian Archives says nothing directly, that similar customs or police raids took place in locations over several States and particularly in Victoria, where three correspondents had been identified. Presumably they also faced customs charges. In New South Wales, however, matters were far worse.

When information on the Adelaide raid was received in Sydney, the local police swooped. Several people were interrogated, no doubt in the manner usual for Commissioner Delaney's police force.

One person, an American teacher, was subsequently charged with two counts of buggery, three of indecent assault on a male person, together with one charge of 'Post Obscene Matter'. The latter charge almost reads like a minor afterthought! He pleaded guilty in the Sydney Quarter Sessions in June 1959 and was sentenced to two years' hard labour. The judge, Mr Justice (later Sir) Adrian Curlewis (well known champion of the Surf Life Saving movement) also ordered that he be deported to America after completion of his sentence.

A second person (whose initials are K.W.), a 36-year-old mail sorter at the GPO, was similarly charged with one count of buggery and two counts of indecent assault and was sentenced to two years' imprisonment. In this case, the matter of Post Obscene Matter was not proceeded with.

K.W.'s flat was searched. Photographic equipment belonging to a third person was found. He turned out to be a 35-year-old cleaner who was later charged with one count of indecent assault. On the latter count, however, he was discharged and so received only a three month sentence for printing an obscene publication.

The investigation now turned overseas. During the course of the Adelaide inquiries 'possession was obtained of a large number of indecent letters and photographs which had been sent by post ... from homosexuals overseas'.

The CIS wrote to the Home Office in London to inform it of their investigations. They sought information on the Popular Pen Friends Club and urged that investigations be carried out by British officials.

Letters were also sent to 'the central authorities of the United States of America, Canada, and Singapore' as well as to the other countries where Brian's correspondents lived. A total of sixteen persons are named in the file — two in the United Kingdom, five in the United States of America, one in Canada, Fiji, and Spain, two in South Africa and one in East Africa and one in France, Algeria and Norway. One assumes that many of them suffered a fate similar to their Australian correspondents. Unfortunately, the file gives no further evidence.

In the following year, 1960, the Police in West Germany were also contacted for information on two other organisations — the publishers of *Cultus* magazine in Amsterdam and the Ruga Studio in Hamburg. Again, the file gives no clue as to subsequent action that may have occurred on this matter. Indeed, at this point information on the case ceases altogether.

The whole story clearly indicates that, during the Cold War period, there was surveillance of the average citizen some in positions of authority. Freedoms which we take for granted nowadays — the right to privacy, the postage of x-rated materials, etc — have only recently been tolerated.

SOURCES: AA (NSW): Commonwealth Investigation Service. ST 2951/1, Correspondence re Criminal Investigations, 1939 — . *item:* N59/1945, Suppression and Traffic in Obscene Publications, part 2

COMING OUT, READY OR NOT

Until September 1970, there was no publicly self-identified lesbian or gay man in Australia. Yet today, with lesbians and gay men so visible in our society, it is sometimes difficult to conceive of a time when gay male sexual behaviour was illegal throughout the country, with people being gaoled as a result; when anti-discrimination legislation was an unheard-of notion; when doctors could unquestioningly carry out aversion therapy, or other medical experiments on homosexuals, with court approval; and when no publicly recognised gay or lesbian community existed in which one could live openly and find support.

How then did all this come about?

The 1960s as the decade of change in Australia, began with the (almost wholesome) concept of 'the teenager' and ended with that of 'the hippie' and 'counter-culture'. The concept of 'liberation', of physical and intellectual freedom and pride in one's self, which came from the Women's Liberation Movement, the black Civil Rights Movement and the Anti-Vietnam War Movement, can generally be said to have politicised the generation of 'the Sixties'.

To the homosexual people of this generation who absorbed these ideas, the concept of gay liberation was embraced as an idea whose time had come.

As we have seen, from 1953 onwards, homosexuality began to be openly discussed in the Australian media and the New South Wales Parliament in the 1955 had even set up its own inquiry into the causes and cures of homosexuality, which never reported.

In Australia, however, none of this led to the rise of a body such as the Homosexual Law Reform Society in England. Similarly, the homophile organisations which existed in the large cities of the United States from the early Fifties — the Mattachine Society and the Daughters of Bilitis — were unknown in Australia.

What did exist was a hidden network of pubs and bars and, from the late 1960s, social groups such as the Knights of Chameleons, The Polynesians and The Boomerangs in Sydney. But these were largely unknown outside the closeted Camp Scene as the homosexual sub-culture by then referred to itself.

One piece, even with its evident self-oppression and the aping of heterosexual life, gives us a clue as to life within the sub-culture. It is a description by journalist John Edwards of a visit to a camp nightclub —

> "Dearly Beloved Brethren," calls the compere, and then he explodes into lilting laughter and can't continue.
> "Dearly beloved brethren," ... he explodes again.
> "Anyhow," he says when he recovers, "Do you Cahill take Tim to be your dearly beloved ... er ... whatever?"
> Cahill gives hushed assent, and the compere adds insinuatingly, "And now who's going to be butch?" Screams of laughter. Encouraged, the compere swings into his routine ... "I won't ask you to be faithful; I know what Camp marriages are like ... Now, Tim, you may kiss Cahill ... Now I want to kiss both of you."
> Tim from Panania and Cahill from Cronulla rush back into the surrounding shadows. As they pass our table someone says, "Congratulations. Tim, I thought you were lovely."
> Tim squeals, "Oh dear, I was that scared I was trembling."
> Marriages are an established ritual in the Camp community, and many are solemnised in camp night-clubs like this one. Sydney has two big camp cabarets, one in the city itself and one in Darlinghurst, which are vibrant on Friday and Saturday nights with hundreds of camps celebrating homosexuality in a society socially and legally hostile to it; they are enchanted caverns for a humdrum group of camp men and women scared by the leering intolerance of weekday society.

A Homosexual Law Reform Society of the Australian Capital Territory was set up in Canberra for some months in 1969 but, while homosexual people were members, the spokespeople were heterosexual. Similarly, the Australian Lesbian Movement, which was established in early 1970 as a chapter of the Daughters of Bilitis, was a closed support group for lesbians in Melbourne with a non-lesbian woman as its spokesperson.

It was, therefore, something of a shock to most Australians to read in *The Australian* of 10 September 1970 of the formation of an organisation, Campaign Against Moral Persecution Incorporated (or CAMP Inc), dedicated to removing the stigma which society still attached to homosexuality. (The name was deliberately chosen to give an Australian flavour to the organisation, 'camp' was a word of self-description within the homosexual community, 'gay' was not.) Even more surprising was the openness of CAMP Inc's founders, John Ware and Christabel Poll, in agreeing to be interviewed and photographed for a feature article, again in *The Australian*, on 19

John Ware and Christabel Poll

September 1970. It took a great deal of courage and the response was extraordinary. In John Ware's own words, 'the media went mad.'

John and Chris had begun in Australia a movement that is still with us. Not that they foresaw these consequences. Indeed their own aims were quite modest. John, particularly, had come out of academic psychiatry where, as a student, he had had difficulties reconciling the established medical view of homosexuality as an illness with the reality of his own life. He was happily settled with a lover, as was Christabel. They both looked to the formation of a small group which would be knowledgeable about current thinking on homosexuality and be able to respond publicly, putting forward a gay viewpoint.

The final decision to found this 'society' followed the reporting in the Australian media of the formation of gay liberation groups in the Untied States following the New York Stonewall riots of 27-29 June 1969, and especially, the reporting of the first anniversary Stonewall/Gay Pride marches which had taken place across America in 1970.

The announcement of the formation of CAMP Inc also brought an unexpected response. It was the extraordinary amount of correspondence the group began to receive which gave the founders some inkling that what they had started might be a little bigger than they had imagined. They sifted through the letters, selected those whose writers seemed at ease with their homosexuality and supported the aims of the society and called a preliminary meeting for 17 November 1970 at Christabell's flat in the Delmont apartment block at Milson's Point, North Sydney. From here the decision was taken to go ahead with a public meeting.

So, on 6 February 1971, the first public gathering of homosexual men and lesbians took place in a small church hall in the suburb of Balmain, then the heart of Sydney's counter-culture. Chris and John were confirmed, more by default than anything else, as convenors and spokespeople and CAMP Inc was properly launched.

By the end of February, other branches of CAMP had formed in Brisbane and in Melbourne (where it was known as Society 5) as well as on the campus of the University of Sydney. By the end of the year, branches had been established in all capital cities and on most campuses. CAMP Inc became known as CAMP NSW.

Each of the organisations was like an umbrella group. Most activity was carried out in the various subgroups concerned with such things as law reform, married gays, religion, and social activities. Eventually counselling was also added to the list of activities.

By the end of 1971, each organisation began to be structured as well. Positions such a secretary and treasurer were agreed on as the organisations became more conventional in their operation (something which John in Sydney also found alien and from which eventually he was glad to step aside.)

Each of the organisations was very much quietly reformist, rather than revolutionary. Quite early on in Sydney, John Ware had stated that it would be years before we saw the first homosexual demonstration in Australia. But in that he was wrong. On 8 October 1971, some 70 people demonstrated outside the Sydney headquarters of the Liberal Party in support of the pre-selection of Tom Hughes, then Federal Attorney-General. He was facing a right-wing challenge from well known homophobe, Jim Cameron, following comments Hughes had made in favour of homosexual law reform. The demonstration was bright and cheerful and marked an important milestone in the history of gay liberation. *CAMP Ink*, the group's magazine, proclaimed, 'October was the month when we came of age, politically.'

Some members of CAMP NSW disagreed. They had become dissatisfied with the 'reformist' approach of the organisation and, in July 1971, formed themselves into a gay liberation cell within CAMP. Already the more radical politics and ideas of the Gay Liberation Front in the United States had begun to come to Australia.

An uneasy relationship began to grow up between this cell and CAMP NSW. Its outspoken radicalism and counter-cultural outlook were alienating to the general membership of CAMP. This was so much the case that at a Sexual Liberation forum at Sydney University in January 1972 (at which Germaine Greer and Dennis Altman were among the speakers), Sydney Gay Liberation (SGL) declared itself a separate organisation. Thus began the political diversity of the gay movement in Australia.

By May 1972, a Gay Liberation Front had been formed in Melbourne and gay liberation groups were established (or replaced Campus Camp) at the University of Sydney, the University of New South Wales, the Australian National University in Canberra, at Melbourne University and later in Perth and Adelaide, where the Gay Activists Alliance formed in 1973.

The style of meeting of these groups, especially SGL, was generally unstructured, indeed chaotic. There was endless discussion, consciousness raising sessions, etc. What was achieved was probably more personal than political. In true counter-culture style, there was contempt for the established political system. Political activity centred on the demonstration and on 'Zaps'. These were activities designed to confront society, and could range from a man appearing in make-up in a public place to street theatre or even the disruption of lectures by aversion therapists (not unlike the activities of ACT-UP today).

The first major demonstration organised by SGL, in July 1972, was outside the Australian Broadcasting Commission offices in Sydney following the management ban on a item on gay liberation going to air on a TV current affairs program. It was notable also for the arrest of David McDiarmid, the first arrest at a gay political demonstration in Australia. Other demonstrations occurred in capitals such as Brisbane and Perth in September. But again it was in Sydney that the real confrontation with police occurred. Seventeen people were arrested at a march in Martin Place. It was a foretaste of similar confrontations to come, the most spectacular of which was to occur at the first Gay Mardi Gras in 1978.

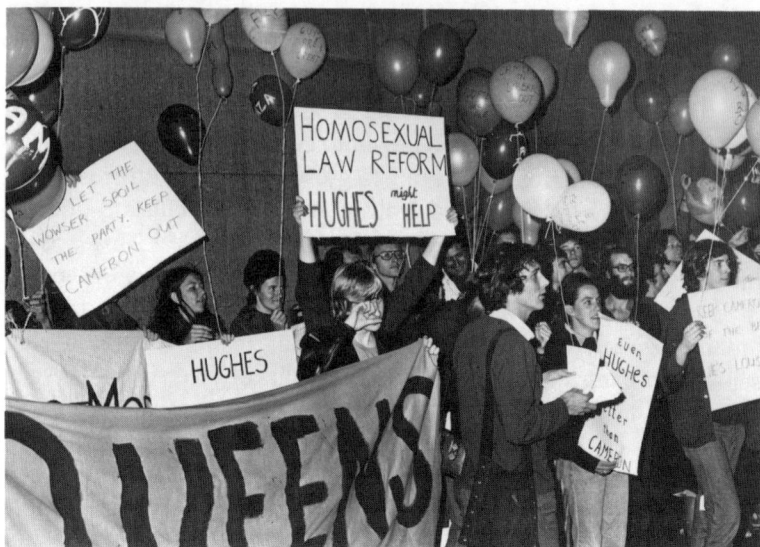

Camping it up at Liberal Party Headquarters

Relations between CAMP and Gay Liberation groups remained strained for the next couple of years. On occasions there was co-operation, such as at the demonstrations outside the Mosman Anglican Church, on Sydney's North shore, following the sacking of the church secretary, Peter Bonsall Boone, after he appeared openly with his lover on the ABC-TV program *Chequerboard*. At other times there was hostility, such as when SGL refused to support the candidature of David Widdup against Prime Minister Billy MacMahon at the December 1972 election (because it smacked of bourgeois politics). David campaigned on the slogan, 'I've got my eye on Billy's seat!'

On one matter the organisations shared a problem — the way men related to women in the movement. Women had been equal and enthusiastic partners in the early workings of both CAMP and Gay Liberation. By early 1973, however, many women were having increasing difficulty coping with the sexist attitudes of many gay men. At the same time, lesbians were attempting to work out their place in a feminist movement also sometimes hostile to them. The upshot was that many turned their energies and involvement to feminist or lesbian separatist organisations or simply drifted away from a gay movement which they felt held little for them. This trend was only reversed in the late 1980s with the beginnings of 'coalition politics'.

If any event could be said to mark the end of this first phase of gay liberation (especially in Sydney) it was the Gay Pride Week celebrations held in Adelaide, Melbourne and Sydney in September 1973. It was almost as if the energy expended in organising the week left little for anything else. This is particularly true of SGL, which folded soon afterwards. People drifted on or into more specialised activities in trades unions, the Australian Union of Students or publishing, with some founding in 1974, *GLP: Gay Liberation Press*.

The various CAMP groups had also changed by 1974. Some women left or drifted away. Other people became involved in their own specialist groups. The changes were also different from state to state. In New South Wales, for example, the counselling side of the organisation came to dominate (and the name of the organisation was later changed to the Gay and Lesbian Counselling Service, a name it retains) while in Western Australia, CAMP remained essentially a political group until it disbanded in the late 1980s.

The early years of gay liberation in Australia were enthusiastic, energetic and spectacular, at least for the participants and, one suspects, a bewildering spectacle for the population and the media at large.

By 1974 practical achievements were few — limited law reform had been enacted in South Australia and, in October 1973, the Federal Parliament had passed a motion in favour of homosexual law reform, though this was more symbolic than practical. But at least one public group, which acted as a focus for activity, had been established in the larger cities as had counselling services. These groups were small and they failed to attract a larger membership from the broader gay community which was increasingly centred on the bar culture. Indeed, in the case of SGL in particular, there was open, and possibly elitist, contempt for 'bar queens'.

With the formation of CAMP Inc in 1970, gay liberation in its broadest sense had been permanently placed on the social agenda not to be removed. 'Coming Out' became not only a personal statement but a political one as well. And the commitment which the activities of those years engendered in many of the participants ensured their involvement, often in their own small way, in the life of the gay and lesbian communities even to today.

SOURCES: FOR EVENTS IN THE UNITED STATES, SEE:
Donn Teal, *The Gay Militants* (New York, 1971)
Dennis Altman, *Homosexual: Oppression and Liberation* (Sydney, 1972)
John D'Emilio, *Sexual Politics, Sexual Communities: The Making of a Homosexual Minority, 1940-1970* (Chicago, 1983)
Martin Duberman, *Stonewall* (New York, 1993)
FOR EVENTS IN THE UNITED KINGOM, SEE:
Jeffrey Weeks, *Coming Out: Homosexual politics in Britain, from the Nineteenth Century to the Present* (London, 1977)
Aubrey Walter (ed), *Coming Out: The Years of Gay Liberation 1970-1974* (London, 1980)
FOR EVENTS IN AUSTRALIA, SEE:
Denise Thompson, *Flaws in the Social Fabric: Homosexuals in Sydney* (Sydney, 1985)
Garry Wotherspoon, *City of the Plain: History of a Gay Sub-culture* (Sydney, 1991)
Robert French, Sue Wills and Ken Davis (eds), *Into the Streets: The Gay Movement in Australia* (Sydney, forthcoming).